And after you have suffered a little while,
the God of all grace, who has called you to his eternal
glory in Christ, will himself restore, confirm,
strengthen, and establish you. To him be
the dominion forever and ever. Amen.

—1 Peter 5:10–11

Resurrection Life in a World of Suffering

Other Books by the Gospel Coalition

Resurrection Life in a World of Suffering

1 Peter

D. A. CARSON

AND

KATHLEEN B. NIELSON,

EDITORS

WHEATON, ILLINOIS

Trade paperback ISBN: 978-1-4335-5700-2
ePub ISBN: 978-1-4335-5703-3
PDF ISBN: 978-1-4335-5701-9
Mobipocket ISBN: 978-1-4335-5702-6

Library of Congress Cataloging-in-Publication Data

Names: Carson, D. A., editor.
Title: Resurrection life in a world of suffering : 1 Peter / Donald A. Carson and Kathleen B. Nielson, editors.
Description: Wheaton : Crossway, 2018. | Includes bibliographical references and index.
Identifiers: LCCN 2017031559 (print) | LCCN 2018018161 (ebook) | ISBN 9781433557019 (pdf) | ISBN 9781433557026 (mobi) | ISBN 9781433557033 (epub) | ISBN 9781433557002 (tp)
Subjects: LCSH: Bible. Peter, 1st--Commentaries--Congresses.
Classification: LCC BS2795.53 (ebook) | LCC BS2795.53 .R47 2018 (print) | DDC 227/.9207--dc23
LC record available at https://lccn.loc.gov/2017031559

Crossway is a publishing ministry of Good News Publishers.

CH			28	27	26	25	24	23	22	21	20	19	18
15	14	13	12	11	10	9	8	7	6	5	4	3	2	1

Contents

Preface

In June 2016, the Gospel Coalition held its third national women's conference—another conference for women but not all about women! We gathered around the Word of God, with plenary sessions of expositional teaching that took us right through the epistle of 1 Peter in three days. It was a rich feast, as we together received the apostle Peter's message of resurrection life in a world of suffering.

This book represents the fruit of that conference, combining the voices of women and men who taught the Word and lifted up the Lord Jesus among us. We delight in this combination of speakers, and we rejoice especially to see women encouraged to study and share the Scriptures together—not just at conferences but even more in and through their local church bodies.

In order to help equip readers to study and share the book of 1 Peter among those to whom they minister, we've included in this volume more than just a transcription of the conference talks. First, we're delighted that Rev. Juan Sanchez, pastor and TGC Council member, was willing to write an introduction that lets us get to know "Peter the expositor." Pastor Sanchez beautifully shows how Peter expounds the Old Testament Scriptures even as he writes the New, setting forth Jesus as the fulfillment of God's eternal purposes. Many of the following chapters refer rather quickly to Old Testament passages quoted or referenced by

Peter, but the introduction carefully demonstrates how the Old Testament context lights up this whole epistle.

Each chapter is followed by reflection questions and by a short section called "Think Like an Expositor," in which we explore some of the process of expositional study and preparation, using comments from the speakers/authors themselves. Finally, the book's conclusion consists of a lively and instructive transcript of a workshop interview from TGCW16, on the subject of studying and teaching 1 Peter.

The epistle of 1 Peter speaks to our time in a piercing way. The believers to whom Peter wrote were a scattered and often scorned minority within an empire where Christians were increasingly unwelcome; direct persecution was on the horizon. Believers today can identify—certainly in parts of the world where persecution of Christians occurs regularly, and also in places where Christians increasingly suffer ridicule and intolerance. Peter's message is one of gospel hope and strengthening grace, all centered in the resurrected Lord Jesus through whom we are born again to a living hope.

May this volume help spread gospel hope—the hope of resurrection life in a world of suffering.

Kathleen Nielson

Introduction

Peter the Expositor: The Apostle's Use of Scripture in 1 Peter

Juan Sanchez

You've likely never heard of the Mystics or the Jays, but they were two musical bands made up of students from the Tuskegee Institute in Alabama. Like most college bands, they didn't last—at least not as the Mystics and the Jays. In 1968 these two groups decided to come together.[1] But, as the story goes, "the members nearly went stir-crazy trying to pick a name for the group, but with no success."[2] Out of frustration, the drummer gave the trumpet player a dictionary and said, "Pick a name."[3] You might more readily know this band as The Commodores, Lionel Richie being its most famous member. Can you imagine making such an important decision as a band's name simply by opening a dictionary, pointing to a page, and choosing the first word that you see? What if the trumpet player had pointed to *commode* instead? "Ladies

---

[1] "Biography," Commodores website, accessed January 18, 2017, http://www.commodoreslive.com/.
[2] "Commodores," Billboard website, accessed January 18, 2017, http://www.billboard.com/artist/299566/commodores/biography.
[3] Ibid.

and gentlemen, put your hands together for The Commodes!" No. That wouldn't work, would it?

Ironically, too many times we approach the Bible in the same way. We may not close our eyes and point to a text, but we might as well. Consider how we "use" the Bible when we take a specific text and directly apply it to ourselves or our situation without any regard for what it meant to the original audience. Because you're reading this book, I believe you want to be a faithful reader, student, and/or teacher of the Bible. But if we are to be faithful in handling God's Word, not only will we need to submit ourselves to its authority; we will also need to understand what a particular passage meant to its original hearers and reflect on how the life, death, resurrection, and exaltation of Christ shed light on our text. Only after following this course should we apply a biblical text to ourselves or our audience.

Knowing that we come to the Bible with various assumptions (gender-related, ethnic, denominational, generational, cultural, etc.), we should aim to allow the Scriptures to speak so that we hear only what the Scriptures say—nothing more, nothing less. In fact, as we read and study God's Word, we should allow Scripture to correct our prejudices and reshape our assumptions whenever necessary. And when we share God's Word with others, whether in a one-on-one situation, a classroom, or a large group, our conviction should simply be to expose what the Bible says. Our word *expositional* or *expository* comes from this conviction. In an expositional or expository message, the point of the text becomes the point of our message, faithfully applied to our hearers.[4]

As we'll see, the apostle Peter shares this same conviction regarding Scripture. Consequently, Peter serves as an excellent guide for how to read our Bibles; he exposes how the Old Testament is fulfilled in Jesus and how it applies to believers under the new covenant in first-century Asia Minor. To understand and learn from

---

[4]I credit Mark Dever with this definition. Dever is the pastor of Capitol Hill Baptist Church in Washington, DC.

how Peter, the expositor, handles Scripture, we will seek to answer four questions: (1) What was Peter's view of Scripture? (2) What did Peter know concerning Scripture? (3) What was Peter's message in 1 Peter? And (4) how did Peter use Scripture in 1 Peter?

Peter's View of Scripture

What we call the Old Testament, Peter, along with Jesus, the other apostles, and the early Christians considered their Scriptures: the Law (the first five books of Moses), the Prophets, and the Writings (sometimes "the Psalms" was used to summarize the Writings). The New Testament identifies the Hebrew Scriptures with a variety of combinations of these three descriptions. For example, Jesus said, "Do not think that I have come to abolish *the Law or the Prophets*; I have not come to abolish them but to fulfill them" (Matt. 5:17). He also said that the whole *Law and the Prophets* depend on the greatest and second greatest commandments: to love God and to love your neighbor as yourself (Matt. 22:40). In fact, Jesus understood his life, death, resurrection, and exaltation as a fulfillment of *the Law of Moses and the Prophets and the Psalms* (Luke 24:44). For this reason, Luke writes that "beginning with Moses and all the Prophets, [Jesus] interpreted to [the two disciples on the road to Emmaus] *in all the Scriptures* the things concerning himself" (Luke 24:27).

As for Peter, even though he walked with Jesus, sat under his teaching, witnessed him heal the sick, and even experienced the display of his glory on the Mount of Transfiguration (2 Pet. 1:16–18), he never dismisses God's written Word. Instead, he argues that what he witnessed with his own eyes and heard with his own ears only confirmed what had already been written in Scripture—the prophetic Word (2 Pet. 1:19). That's why Peter encourages his readers to "pay attention" to this prophetic Word, because "no prophecy was ever produced by the will of man, but men spoke from God as they were carried along by the Holy Spirit" (2 Pet. 1:21). Here is Peter's view of divine inspiration:

God spoke through individuals as they were "carried along" by the Holy Spirit.

To be sure, divine inspiration did not end when the Old Testament was completed. Peter and the other New Testament writers were conscious that, under the inspiration of the Holy Spirit, they too were writing Scripture. For example, Peter acknowledges that, though some of the apostle Paul's writings were hard to understand, they were Scripture nonetheless (2 Pet. 3:16). So, then, not only did Peter view what we call the "Old Testament" as divinely inspired and authoritative; in writing his first letter to the Christians in Asia Minor, he too was under divine inspiration. What Peter says in 1 Peter, God says. But just what did Peter know concerning his Bible?

Peter's Knowledge of Scripture

It should not be surprising that in light of Peter's view of Scripture, he knew his Bible well. But not only did Peter have a thorough understanding of the content of the Law, the Prophets, and the Writings; he understood that it all pointed to a greater reality that was fulfilled in Jesus Christ. For Peter, then, the story of Israel does not merely serve as a source for quotations and illustrations. It is the backdrop against which he presents his message to the Christians in Asia Minor.

Peter knew that God created humanity as his image with the express purpose of reflecting his glory and representing his rule on the earth (Genesis 1–2). But Adam and Eve rebelled against God's rule. And because God is holy and just, he punished them by removing them from his presence. Apart from God, they began to experience increasing sin, rebellion, chaos, and eventual death (Genesis 3). As human sinfulness increased (Genesis 4–5), so did God's judgment, but so also did God's grace (Genesis 6–11).

Peter also knew that, despite Adam's rebellion, God raised up Israel to reflect his glory and represent his rule over the earth. The story of Israel as a nation began with Abraham. Through this man

God would bless the world (Gen. 12:1–3). Abraham's name would be great, and he would become a great nation. Nationhood indicates many descendants, and this many people required a land to dwell in. God promised to provide all these to Abraham (Gen. 12:1–2). The rest of the world would find either blessing or curse based on how they responded to God's chosen one (Gen. 12:3).

By the end of Genesis, God's promise of descendants was fulfilled (Ex. 1:1–7); however, a king ascended to the Egyptian throne who did not know Abraham's descendants. Because he feared their numbers, the new king enslaved them and tried to put an end to their strength. Israel was far from the land God had promised them, and they were in no position to do anything about it. To address the obstacle to obtaining the land, God rescued Israel by his mighty hand (Ex. 12:29–42), and he brought them to himself at Mount Sinai in order to establish the foundation of his relationship with them in a covenant (Exodus 19–24). God reminded Israel that, though the entire world belongs to him, he chose them out of all the nations of the world as his special treasure, his treasured possession (Ex. 19:5). Exodus 19:6 explains what it means to be God's special treasure: Israel was to be a royal priesthood (kingdom of priests) and a holy nation.

As a royal priesthood, Israel had special access to God's presence, and they were to serve as mediators to the surrounding nations, showing them what it was like to live under God's rule. As a holy nation, they were to dedicate themselves solely to God; and this dedication to God would result in a separation from the world. By their holiness, they would provide a witness to the surrounding nations that God alone was their king and that they alone were citizens of his kingdom rule. They were to be distinct from the world in their worship, their dress, their diet, their morality, their sexual practices, their work—everything. By these distinctions, they would show how different was their God from the gods of the surrounding nations and what it was like to live under his gracious rule and care. As they displayed God's morality and concern for one another, particularly the least among them, they would display to the world the compassion of their God and his kingdom citizens.

Peter knew that God confirmed this special relationship with Israel in a covenant, because this was the covenant that, as a faithful Jew, he had been taught to obey. Exodus 20–24, the Book of the Covenant, explains the obligations of both God and Israel in this relationship. Such covenants also indicated that if either party breached the agreement, the penalty was death. For this reason, blood was often a part of covenant ceremonies. This is precisely what takes place in Exodus 24:7–8. Moses read the Book of the Covenant in the hearing of the people; the people agreed to obey; Moses sprinkled blood on the people, thus consecrating or separating them out of the world for God; and, finally, Moses declared, "Behold the blood of the covenant that the LORD has made with you in accordance with all these words" (Ex. 24:8).

Unfortunately, Peter also knew that the story of Israel was littered with repeated violations of this covenant. Israel entered the land promised by God under Joshua's leadership (book of Joshua), but it was not until they came under the leadership of King David that they were truly established in the land (1–2 Samuel). Unfortunately, with the exception of a few kings, David's sons did not live up to David's name. As a result, the kingdom was torn in two (930 BC). Ten tribes traveled north and established a capital in Samaria, while two tribes, Judah and Benjamin, remained in the south. Because of repeated covenant violations, the two kingdoms began a downward spiral toward destruction (1–2 Kings; 1–2 Chronicles). Though God was slow to anger, in 722 BC God put an end to the northern kingdom by the hands of the Assyrians. And finally, in 587/586 BC, God sent the Babylonians to conquer Jerusalem. In both instances, the people of God were exiled to a foreign land.

Because of the prophetic writings, though, Peter, along with every other Jew, held out hope for the restoration of Israel. Even before the exiles, the prophets announced that God would do something new, something never seen before. God himself would shepherd his people by raising up a faithful shepherd from King David's line (Jer. 23:1–6; Ezek. 34:1–24; 37:15–28). And God would lead them in a second exodus that would make them forget that the first one had ever happened (Isa. 43:1–19; see also Jer. 23:7–8). All this God would accomplish on the basis of a new covenant, a new relationship (Isaiah 54–56), established on the substitutionary death of the Lord's faithful, suffering servant (Isa. 52:13–53:12). This new covenant would grant God's people a new heart, God's Spirit, and forgiveness of sins; in other words, they would be empowered to obey God (Jer. 31:31–34; Ezek. 36:22–27). The blessings of this covenant would result in a special relationship with God and abundant blessing in his presence (Ezek. 36:28–38).

God promised to return Israel to their land after the exile (Jer. 29:10). But during their exile, Israel was to be a blessing while living in Babylon, seeking the welfare of the city by praying for it, because "in its welfare you will find your welfare" (Jer. 29:7). While in Babylon, Israel was to "build houses and live in them; plant gardens and eat their produce" (Jer. 29:5). God also commanded them: "Take wives and have sons and daughters; take wives for your sons, and give your daughters in marriage, that they may bear sons and daughters; multiply there, and do not decrease" (Jer. 29:6). At the end of seventy years, God raised up Cyrus, king of Persia, to release Israel to return to the land, beginning in 539 BC (2 Chron. 36:22). The Jews rebuilt the temple (book of Ezra) and the city wall (book of Nehemiah), but it became clear that this was not the promised restoration that they had hoped for (Ezra 3:12–13). Something else, some greater restoration was sure to come (Hag. 2:6–9).

By grouping Jesus's genealogy from Abraham to David (Matt. 1:2–6a), from David to the Babylonian exile (Matt. 1:6b–11), and from the Babylonian exile to Jesus's birth (Matt. 1:12–16), our

New Testament opens by presenting Jesus as the answer to the Babylonian exile: fourteen generations from Abraham to David, fourteen generations "from David to the deportation to Babylon," and fourteen generations from "the deportation to Babylon to the Christ" (Matt. 1:17). There is a sense, then, that while Jesus has come to rescue his people from the exile once and for all, they are still in exile on this earth until Jesus consummates the kingdom. Peter knew this and picks up on this idea when he calls the Christians in Asia Minor "elect exiles of the Dispersion" (1 Pet. 1:1) and ends his letter with greetings from "She [the church] who is at Babylon" (1 Pet. 5:13). For Peter, then, the Christians in Asia Minor, along with all Christians everywhere, are the people of God in exile awaiting the final restoration of all things.

Peter's Message in 1 Peter

If we're to understand 1 Peter, we need to understand something about the world of the Christians in Asia Minor in the first century, Peter's original audience.[5] There is no evidence that Peter wrote his first letter during a time of empire-wide persecution, but it is clear that these Christian brothers and sisters were suffering for what they believed. In this sense, we can say that the experience of the Christians in 1 Peter is much like that of Christians in the West today. Unlike some of our brothers and sisters in other parts of the world who face persecution in the form of war, violence, displacement, torture, and even death, we face cultural discrimination, social pressures, and the potential loss of rights and privileges simply for identifying with Christ. Peter's readers faced similar pressures, and he writes to encourage them to endure faithfully under these circumstances because "after you have suffered a little while, the God of all grace, who has called you to his eternal glory in Christ, will himself restore, confirm, strengthen, and establish you" (5:10).

---

[5] You may gain much of this information in a good commentary, Bible dictionary, or Bible encyclopedia.

We can summarize Peter's message in 1 Peter in four words: *salvation, holiness, suffering,* and *perseverance.* Peter encourages the Christians in Asia Minor to endure suffering faithfully by looking back at the great salvation God has accomplished for them in Christ and looking forward to the future inheritance that awaits them (1:1–12). While on this earth, though, they are sojourners and exiles called to live holy lives in order to provide a faithful witness to the unbelieving world around them (1:13–3:7). And like Christ, they too will suffer. But with Christ, if they endure faithfully, they will share in his victory, vindication, and glory (3:8–4:19). Until then, Peter's readers are to persevere together under the faithful leadership of elders (5:1–5), as they humble themselves, cast their anxieties upon Jesus, remain in sober watchfulness, and resist the Devil (5:6–11).

Peter's Use of Scripture in 1 Peter

We don't have space to identify every time Peter uses the Old Testament in 1 Peter, but we can identify and explain enough references to understand how Peter uses Scripture to encourage his readers to endure faithfully. To be sure, the New Testament authors' use of the Old Testament raises several questions,[6] but for our purposes, let's keep it simple. It will be easiest to identify Peter's use of the Old Testament in 1 Peter when he directly quotes the Old Testament. When he does, he cites either a Hebrew text or a Greek translation (the Septuagint, LXX). In many of our English translations, these Old Testament citations are italicized or set apart in a way that we may recognize them easily enough (see 1:24–25; 2:6–8; 3:10–12; 4:18). In at least one

---

[6] Some questions are: How do we know when they reference an Old Testament passage if it's not a direct quotation? When they paraphrase an Old Testament text that is used often in the Old Testament, which one are they referencing? Or, when they use Old Testament language, how can we be certain they are in fact referencing an Old Testament text? If you're interested in exploring these questions in general, I recommend G. K. Beale, *Handbook on the New Testament Use of the Old Testament: Exegesis and Interpretation* (Grand Rapids, MI: Baker, 2012). If you're interested in how each New Testament author is using the Old Testament Scriptures, then I recommend *Commentary on the New Testament Use of the Old Testament,* ed. G. K. Beale and D. A. Carson (Grand Rapids, MI: Baker, 2007).

instance Peter identifies the citation as Scripture: "For it stands in Scripture . . ." (2:6).

At other times Peter simply alludes to an Old Testament text. Undoubtedly, an allusion is not as easy to identify as a quotation because it is not a direct citation. But often, an allusion sufficiently resembles an Old Testament text or passage to enable us to identify what Old Testament passage it is referring to.[7] For example, the language in chapter 2, verse 9, of "a royal priesthood, a holy nation, a people for his own possession" is so similar to what the Old Testament says of Israel in Exodus 19:6 that there is no question, in my mind, that Peter uses the same language and applies it to his readers. So, with these explanations in mind, and using the four words mentioned above (*salvation*, *holiness*, *suffering*, and *perseverance*), let's work through 1 Peter to see how the apostle uses the story of Israel to encourage the Christians in Asia Minor.

Exile: The Context for 1 Peter

Peter begins his first letter by addressing his readers as the "elect exiles of the Dispersion" (1:1). This language reminds us of Israel under exile. In the closing of the letter, Peter sends greetings from "She who is at Babylon" (5:13). Peter is likely in Rome, the center of power and government in his day, just as Babylon was the center of power and government at the time of the exile of Israel's southern kingdom. The entire context of 1 Peter, then, is one of exile, particularly, the Babylonian exile. Peter wants his readers to understand that because they have identified with Christ, they too are "sojourners and exiles" on this earth (2:11), just as those exiled to Babylon under the power and government of King Nebuchadnezzar in the early 500s BC.

Since they don't belong to this world, the Christians in Asia Minor are likely to face discrimination and persecution at a number of levels. Their own government may take away their rights

---

[7] Beale, *Handbook on the New Testament Use of the Old Testament*, 31.

and privileges (2:13–17). Those under authority could potentially be taken advantage of by those in authority over them (2:18–25). Even Christian wives might face discrimination in their own homes from their unbelieving husbands (3:1–6), while Christian husbands may be tempted not to live with their unbelieving wives in a considerate manner (3:7).

Salvation

1 Peter 1:1–2. During their suffering, Peter encourages his readers to look back at the great salvation the triune God has accomplished for them in Christ and to look forward to the time when this salvation will finally be revealed at the return of Christ. Echoing the covenant ceremony in Exodus 24:3–8, where God defined his relationship with Israel under the old covenant, Peter reminds his readers that they are the people of God with whom God established the promised new covenant. They are not merely exiles; they are "elect" exiles. In other words, they are God's chosen people. God the Father chose them according to his foreknowledge, his prior love before they even existed (1:2a). Now, this is love! It's not based on anything in them; it's based on God's free choice. And the Holy Spirit applied this salvation to them when he set them apart "in . . . sanctification" (1:2b). Just like Israel of old was consecrated or set apart to God at Sinai in Exodus 24, so too Peter's readers were set apart by the Holy Spirit.

But notice that they were set apart to God for a purpose, "for obedience to Jesus Christ and for sprinkling with his blood" (1:2c). Again, just like that covenant ceremony in Exodus 24 when Moses sprinkled Israel with the blood of the covenant, so too the new-covenant people of God were sprinkled with the blood of Jesus, the blood of the new and better covenant. Throughout 1 Peter, I understand him to use the language of "obedience" primarily for that initial obedience of faith to the gospel. This is saving faith. Of course, as we'll see below, initial obedience leads to ongoing obedience.

So, Peter begins his first letter by establishing his readers' identity as the new-covenant people of God, saved and secured by the triune God. The Father chose them; the Son accomplished their salvation by his blood; and the Spirit applied this salvation to all who believed the gospel. As Peter's readers persevered in hope of this salvation, they were sojourning toward an inheritance that is "imperishable, undefiled, and unfading, kept in heaven for you, who by God's power are being guarded through faith for a salvation ready to be revealed in the last time" (1:4–5). Suffering Christians everywhere, then, are encouraged to endure faithfully now by looking back to this great salvation accomplished for us by the triune God and by looking forward with hope to the time when we will receive our eternal inheritance at Christ's return.

1 Peter 1:10–12. Peter also used the Prophets in a general way to remind his readers that, though they may lose rights and privileges as exiles on this earth, they are a privileged people because they live in a privileged time and experience a privileged salvation (1:10–12). Peter tells his readers that the Old Testament prophets "prophesied about the grace that was to be [theirs]" and that they "searched and inquired carefully, inquiring what person or time the Spirit of Christ in them was indicating when he predicted the sufferings of Christ and the subsequent glories" (1:10–11). In other words, the prophets were looking for Christ, and they were longing for the time when he would appear, because they understood that his sufferings would lead to his people's salvation and glory. It was through this promised Christ that the restoration of Israel would come.

Though Peter doesn't cite a specific prophecy, consider just one: Isaiah 53. There is no clearer gospel declaration in the entire Old Testament. Peter reminds his readers that though they may wish to escape suffering and live in a different time, the Old Testament prophets understood that they were serving not themselves, but them: the Christians in Asia Minor and all other Christians under the new covenant (1:12).

We too may wish to live in a different time, an easier time, but Peter reminds us that we are living in a privileged time, and we have experienced a privileged salvation—a salvation the prophets longed for, a salvation that angels marvel over (1:12). Because we are God's chosen new-covenant exiles sojourning on this earth, we endure Christian suffering now by setting our "hope fully on the grace that will be brought to [us] at the revelation of Jesus Christ" (1:13). But what does waiting faithfully for the revelation of Jesus Christ look like for the Christian?

Holiness

1 Peter 1:16. Having been set apart by the Holy Spirit for initial obedience to the gospel, Peter reminds his readers that they are also set apart for ongoing obedience. Once again, Peter uses the story of Israel as a backdrop for the Christian story. Just as Israel was to be holy because God is holy, so too Peter's readers are to be holy because "he who called you is holy" (1:15). Peter grounds his command to be holy in the Levitical command, "You shall be holy, for I am holy" (1:16). Although this command is found in various forms in Leviticus (11:44; 19:2; 20:7, 26), D. A. Carson suggests that Peter cites Leviticus 19:2 exactly from a Greek translation of the Old Testament (LXX, Septuagint).[8] This citation, then, comes from the Holiness Code (Leviticus 11–26) that contains the laws which taught Israel how to maintain distinction from the surrounding nations in relation to various issues: diet (chap. 11), leprosy (chaps. 13–14), sexual morality (chap. 18), loving your neighbor (chap. 19), regulating worship (chaps. 17, 20–22), and celebrating special feast days (chaps. 23–26). The Holiness Code also contained the promise of forgiveness of sin based on an atoning, substitute sacrifice (Leviticus 16).

So, in this brief citation of Leviticus 19:2 in 1:16, Peter brings this entire Levitical code to mind as a background for the holiness

---

[8] D. A. Carson, "1 Peter," in *Commentary on the New Testament Use of the Old Testament*, 1017.

of his readers. Just as Israel was to be different from the surrounding nations to provide a witness to the holiness of their God and the joy of living under his rule, so too Peter's readers worship the same God. He is still holy. And like Israel of old, they are to be holy because God is holy.

To be sure, Peter does not simply place new-covenant Christians under the old-covenant Holiness Code. That would be to put old wine into new wineskins. Still, the foundation of the Levitical code remains the same—love God and love your neighbor as yourself. So, just as the Holiness Code instructed Israel how to be different from their pagan neighbors to witness to the holiness of their God, so too Peter's readers are to be different from their world to witness to the holiness of their God, the same God as Israel's. That's why Peter urges them "as sojourners and exiles to abstain from the passions of the flesh, which wage war against your soul. Keep your conduct among the Gentiles honorable, so that when they speak against you as evildoers, they may see your good deeds and glorify God on the day of visitation" (2:11–12). The Christian's "holiness code" is tied to the new covenant and is revealed in our New Testament. We are to obey all that Jesus has commanded us (Matt. 28:20). For the Christians in Asia Minor, this included submission of citizens to the governing authorities (2:13–17), of slaves to masters (2:18–25), and of believing wives to unbelieving husbands (3:1–6), among other things.

1 Peter 1:19. Not only were Peter's readers to be holy because God is holy; they were to be holy because God had delivered them from their slavery to former sinful ways (1:18a). God purchased their freedom, "not with perishable things such as silver or gold, but with the precious blood of Christ, like that of a lamb without blemish or spot" (1:18b–19). The inheritance of sin from their forefathers points back, ultimately, to our forefather Adam (Genesis 3). Redemption from slavery by the blood of an unblemished lamb reminds us of Israel's bondage in Egypt (Ex. 12:5–7; Deut. 7:8), but it also points to Old Testament language of deliverance from exile (Isa. 52:3).

Before the initial obedience of faith to the gospel, all are enslaved to sin. Peter reminds his readers that at that time, they walked in futile ways, "living in sensuality, passions, drunkenness, orgies, drinking parties, and lawless idolatry" (4:3). But because they were purchased with the precious blood of Christ (1:19), they are now to "live as people who are free, not using [their] freedom as a cover-up for evil, but living as servants [or better yet, *slaves*] of God" (2:16). Having been freed from sin's slavery, Christians are now free to obey God and pursue holiness.

1 Peter 1:24–25. Not only are Peter's readers freed to pursue holiness because of God's deliverance; they are also empowered to obey God, pursue holiness, and love one another because they have been born again by the imperishable seed, "through the living and abiding word of God" (1:23). To emphasize the enduring nature of the word of God as the foundation for the new birth, Peter quotes verses 6 and 8 of Isaiah 40 (1:24–25).

In order to understand how Peter uses Isaiah 40:6 in 1:24–25, we need to understand the context of these words in Isaiah 40. In Isaiah 39, God announces the coming Babylonian invasion and the consequent exile of the Jews. Immediately after his word of judgment, God calls on three voices to announce words of comfort to his people in Jerusalem (Isa. 40:1–2).[9] The first voice calls for the Lord's way to be prepared, because he would come and rescue his people from exile, revealing his glory for all to see (Isa. 40:3–5). The second voice announces that while human life is transient (Isa. 40:6–7), "the word of our God will stand forever" (Isa. 40:8). Finally, the last voice announces that the Lord would come in might, and he would shepherd his people, gathering them in his arms, carrying them in his bosom, and gently leading those who are with young (Isa. 40:9–11). After the announcement of exile, then, God

---

[9] For a helpful explanation of Isa. 40:1–12, see J. Alec Motyer, *The Prophecy of Isaiah: An Introduction and Commentary* (Downers Grove, IL: InterVarsity Press, 1993), 298–302.

comforts his people by reminding them that he himself is coming to rescue them and shepherd them.

What is stunning is that by quoting Isaiah 40, verses 6 and 8, Peter declares that the words meant to comfort the exiles in Isaiah 40 are the words of the gospel that was preached to his readers (1 Pet. 1:25). In other words, the gospel is the announcement of God's coming to rescue his people from exile and shepherd them as a faithful, caring shepherd. We shouldn't be surprised by this application, because the Gospels apply Isaiah 40:3–5 to John the Baptist, who prepared the way for the Lord's promised coming in Jesus (Matt. 3:3; Mark 1:3; Luke 3:4; John 1:23). For now, the Christians in Asia Minor are in exile, as are we, but we have experienced the promised new birth. So, as we Christians await the return of Christ in order to obtain our eternal inheritance, we are empowered to obey God's commands—to "love one another earnestly from a pure heart" (1:22) because God's enduring word was preached to us, and we have experienced the new birth that comes by this enduring word.

1 Peter 2:3. Of course, those who receive the gospel and its promises are to continue to grow in salvation by craving both the enduring word and the Lord himself (2:2), precisely because we have already "tasted that the Lord is good" (2:3). In 2:3 Peter references Psalm 34:8. Psalm 34 is David's response to God's deliverance when he acted as a madman to escape Achish, king of Gath (1 Sam. 21:10–15).[10] The psalm is in two parts. In part 1, verses 1–10, David calls others to join him in praising God for his deliverance. Because David experienced God's deliverance personally (vv. 6–7), he invites all who would believe to experience God's goodness for themselves: "taste and see that the LORD is good" (v. 8a). And, of course, all who "take refuge in him" are blessed (v. 8b).

Peter uses this verse, but he states it in the past tense: "if indeed you have tasted that the Lord is good" (1 Pet. 2:3). In other words,

---

[10] The title of the psalm names Abimelech instead of Achish, but Abimelech simply means "my father is king," so the different name does not necessarily pose a discrepancy.

the Christians in Asia Minor, as the new-covenant people of God set apart by the Holy Spirit for salvation, have indeed experienced God's deliverance. As a result, they are to put away "all malice and all deceit and hypocrisy and envy and all slander" (2:1) by growing in their experience of both the enduring word (1:22–25) and the Lord himself. By longing for Jesus, they would continue to "grow up into salvation" (2:2).

1 Peter 2:6–10. One of the harsh realities Christians will face as exiles in this evil world is the rejection of the world—rejection even from those who are closest to us. This is especially the case for those who come to faith in Christ out of another faith background. Regardless, any rejection is hard to stomach. As Christians weigh the temptation to deny Christ in order to gain the approval of the world, we need to hear Peter's argument in 2:6–10. Peter begins by reminding his readers that when they came to Christ, they came to a Savior who was rejected by his own people (2:4a). And yet he was precious in God's sight (2:4b). To confirm God's choice of this Savior rejected by men, Peter quotes Isaiah 28:16. The context of Isaiah 28 is one of judgment against Ephraim (the northern kingdom) and Jerusalem (the southern kingdom). In arrogance, Israel rejected God's simple teaching (Isa. 28:9–10). Consequently, Israel would experience God's judgment when they heard complicated sounds coming from a "people of strange lips and with a foreign tongue" (Isa. 28:11). This judgment points to the coming invasion of foreigners that would result not only in Israel's destruction but in the exile of its people.

But judgment is never the final word. God himself would lay a foundation stone in Zion, the restored city of God (Isa. 28:16). This stone is precious to God, and Peter clarifies that it is chosen by God (2:6). While Israel refused to believe God's simple message (Isa. 28:1–13) and to hear God's word (Isa. 28:14–15), those who do believe and hear his word "will not be in haste" (Isa. 28:16). Or as Peter clarifies, those who believe will not be put to shame (2:6). That is, they will not be ashamed when God comes in judgment.

Instead, those who believe receive honor (2:7a). But for those who do not believe, Jesus, the stone they rejected, has become the cornerstone (2:7b; see Ps. 118:22) and "a stone of stumbling, and a rock of offense" (2:8; see Isa. 8:14). Peter strings these Old Testament passages together to encourage his readers, reminding them that they have identified with a Savior who has also been rejected by his very people. Jesus is a stumbling block, a rock of offense to "both houses of Israel" (Isa. 8:14). But those who refuse to believe have rejected the very stone God has chosen as a cornerstone to build his new temple (Ps. 118:22).

In other words, though Jesus has been rejected by men, as the cornerstone of the new temple he is vindicated by God. Now, God is building his temple on Jesus, the living stone, by adding all who believe as living stones in this new temple (2:4–5). So, while Christians may be rejected by the world that also rejects Jesus Christ, when judgment comes it is those who refused to believe who will be put to shame, not those who believed. Those who believe will be vindicated just as he has been.

In 2:9–10 Peter explains, at least in part, the honor that his hearers have as "a people for [God's] own possession" (2:9). Peter's use of Isaiah 43:20–21 and Exodus 19:6 in 2:9 is interesting. Isaiah 43 highlights Israel's salvation (return from exile) in the language of a new exodus: "When you pass through the waters, I will be with you" (Isa. 43:2). God promised to gather his scattered people from the four corners of the earth (Isa. 43:5–7) and judge the Babylonians in similar fashion as he had the Egyptians (Isa. 43:16–17). In this new exodus, God would "make a way in the wilderness and rivers in the desert." And God would "give water . . . to give drink to *my chosen people*" (Isa. 43:19–20). Those whom God promised to save are "the people whom I formed for myself *that they might declare my praise*" (Isa. 43:21). Peter then applies the language of Exodus 19:6 ("a royal priesthood, a holy nation, a people for his own possession") to his readers and places it between verses 20 and 21 of Isaiah 43. By doing this, Peter identifies his readers as the people of the second exodus, and like the people of the first exodus, God has saved them to represent him and his kingdom to the unbelieving world.

As a royal priesthood (priest-kings), Israel had a special relationship with God; only they had special access to God's presence. At first this was seen in the tabernacle, the tent where God lived in their midst as they journeyed to the Promised Land. Later, God manifested his presence in the temple in Jerusalem. As the new-covenant people of God, Peter's readers have the honor not only of special access to God's presence; through Christ, they are now the very temple of God—the place where God dwells (2:4–5).

In addition, as priests, Israel was to represent God and his rule/kingdom on the earth to the surrounding nations. To accomplish this representative role, God promised to place them in the center of their world and dwell with them in the land. There they were to serve as mediators to the world, offering a powerful witness to the holiness of their God and life under his rule. Essentially, they were inviting the rest of the world to enter God's kingdom by becoming worshipers of their God. So, then, one of the ways Israel was to relate to the nations was incorporation.[11] However, the prophets spoke of a time when Israel would relate to the rest of the world through an end-time gathering of the nations (Isaiah 56). By applying this language to his readers, Peter indicates that they are the new Israel, the Israel of the second exodus by whom God gathers the nations. However, new-covenant Israel is not located in only one geographic location with one central place of worship; it is located throughout the world, each church serving as an embassy of God's kingdom. As ambassadors, Christians are called "to proclaim the excellencies of him who called you out of darkness into his marvelous light" (2:9). By this proclamation, we are participating in the end-time gathering of the nations to God.

---

[11] Charles H. H. Scobie, "Israel and the Nations: An Essay in Biblical Theology," *Tyndale Bulletin* 43.2 (1992): 286.

To drive the point home that his readers are the new, restored Israel, Peter references Hosea 1:6, 9, 10. Though they were formerly not part of the people of God under the old covenant, through God's call out of darkness, Peter's readers, in fact all Christians, have now become the people of God (2:10). The world may ridicule and reject Christians, but God is building his house, his temple, on the foundation of Jesus Christ. All who respond to his call are built on this foundation. And we, gathered together as local churches, display the glory and holiness of our God by our life together as exiles. For this reason, Peter exhorts: "Keep your conduct among the Gentiles honorable, so that when they speak against you as evildoers, they may see your good deeds and glorify God on the day of visitation" (2:12).

1 Peter 2:24–25; 3:6. As to the question of how the holiness of the new-covenant people of God is to be worked out and displayed in this present evil world, Peter points out several examples. First, Peter urges his readers that despite potential government discrimination or persecution, they are to submit to governing authorities (2:13–17).

Second, Peter reminds his readers that those among them who are servants are to submit to their masters, whether they are just or unjust (2:18–25). For a picture of submission to unjust masters, Peter turns to Christ's example from Isaiah 53 (2:22–25). Jesus was righteous, without sin, yet he suffered at the hands of those in authority over him (Isa. 53:9). When Jesus was mocked and ridiculed, he did not return evil for evil (Isa. 53:7). In fact, Jesus suffered faithfully unto death, bearing our sins (Isa. 53:4), being "pierced for our transgressions" and "crushed for our iniquities" (Isa. 53:5). As a result, we find healing, salvation by his wounds (Isa. 53:5). And, of course, we needed to be saved because we were like wandering sheep who had strayed from their master (Isa. 53:6). But, Peter tells his readers, they "have now returned to the Shepherd and Overseer of [their] souls" (2:25).

Finally, Peter reminds wives married to unbelieving husbands that "as Sarah obeyed Abraham" (3:6), they too are to follow their husband's leadership with a quiet humility (3:1–5). Peter's reference to Sarah is from Genesis 18:12. Sarah has just heard the angel of the Lord tell Abraham that she would have a child; listening in, she laughs out loud because she thinks she is too old to bear children. The irony of the allusion is that Sarah shows respect to her husband by calling him "lord," even while expressing unbelief and even while not in her husband's presence. Women who follow Sarah's example are her daughters, showing respect to their husbands. Such submission is beautiful before God (3:4) and may possibly even win an unbelieving husband to Christ (3:1).[12]

Suffering

1 Peter 3:10–12. Because we identify with Christ, we are sojourners and exiles in this world. And because we are different from this world, we will be persecuted. As Jesus said, "If you were of the world, the world would love you as its own" (John 15:19). But the question Christians face is, when suffering comes because of our identity with Christ, how are we to suffer so that we maintain our faithful witness to King Jesus? First, Peter says, Christians are not to repay evil for evil (3:9); instead, we are to bless those who persecute us that we may obtain a blessing (3:10; see also Matt. 5:11–12).

Peter grounds his argument in Psalm 34:12–16. As we saw above, the setting of Psalm 34 is God's deliverance of David before King Achish. While the first part of the psalm (vv. 1–10) is David's invitation to experience God's deliverance, part 2 (vv. 11–22) is David's invitation to learn wisdom (the fear of the Lord) from him. Psalm 34:12–16 contains biblical wisdom—instruction on how to maintain covenant faithfulness. But verses 17–18 offer a promise:

---

[12] It is important to note that submission to any authority is not blind. I suspect that these issues will be addressed as each text is worked out through this book. We are to follow those in authority over us so long as they do not command us to do things contrary to God's will. If the choice is between obeying God or man, it is better to obey God.

When the righteous cry for help, the LORD hears
    and delivers them out of all their troubles.
The LORD is near to the brokenhearted
    and saves the crushed in spirit.

As Peter's readers faced suffering, they were to endure it, not by repaying evil for evil, but by repaying evil with good. The reason? Because God will hear their cries, and he will deliver them "out of them all" (Ps. 34:19). "None of those who take refuge in him will be condemned" (Ps. 34:22).

Of course, Peter does not mean that God protects his people from every instance of physical suffering, or in any instance, for that matter. God's salvation means that even in death, God will deliver his people to himself, where we will receive our eternal inheritance. As Peter says, it may be necessary for Christians to endure through various trials for the testing of their faith, but such endurance will "result in praise and glory and honor at the revelation of Jesus Christ" (1:7).

1 Peter 3:18–22. Admittedly, in 3:18–22 we come to the most difficult section of 1 Peter. However, if we focus on what we know, I think we can understand Peter's point. Notice the trajectory of Jesus's path. Christ, the righteous one, suffered, was put to death (in the body), and made alive (in the realm of the Spirit)—resurrection (3:18). That's clear enough! Then Jesus was exalted to the heavenly Father's right hand (3:22). So, this is Jesus's path: righteous suffering, death, resurrection, and exaltation to glory. Peter encourages his readers by reminding them that in the midst of righteous suffering, this is their path as well.

The hard part is trying to discern what happened between Jesus's resurrection (3:19) and his exaltation (3:22). In 3:19–20, I understand Peter to be referring to Genesis 6, where "the sons of God saw that the daughters of man were attractive. And they took as their wives any they chose" (Gen. 6:2). In 1 Peter 3:19 Jesus preaches to the imprisoned spirits after his resurrection. I understand this passage to say that Jesus announced to these imprisoned spirits his victory over sin, death, the Devil, and even them.[13] As we put all this together, then, it is clear that Peter encourages the suffering Christians in Asia Minor with the victory of Jesus Christ. Yes, we will share in his sufferings, but we will also share in his victory!

But Peter is not done. He continues the theme of Noah (Genesis 6–9) to remind his readers that in the same way that God saved Noah and his family through the waters of judgment, so now baptism paints a picture of salvation through judgment. Just as in Noah's day, God will bring us through the outpouring of his wrath on this sinful world at final judgment. Looking back at our baptism now reminds us that because we have been united with Christ in baptism, we are not only united to Christ in his suffering and death, but we are also united to Christ in his resurrection (3:21), exaltation, and glory. The pathway of suffering *is* the pathway to victory, vindication, and glory. But in order to share in Jesus's victory, we must persevere until the end.

Perseverance

1 Peter 4:17–18. While suffering as exiles on this earth, we persevere by arming ourselves with the mind of Christ (4:1). We're not to lose our heads when we face Christian suffering (4:7), nor should we be surprised when it happens (4:12). Instead, we are to endure suffering in the fear of God, knowing that judgment will begin with God's people (4:17). The allusion is to Ezekiel 9:6, where God warns that he will begin judging the idolaters among his people, beginning at his sanctuary. To bolster his argument, in 4:18 Peter cites Proverbs 11:31: "If the righteous is scarcely saved, what will become of the ungodly and the sinner?" Peter reminds his readers that one of the purposes of suffering, in God's providence,

---

[13] Again, I take this "preaching" to have occurred after Jesus's resurrection. For my explanation of this passage, see Juan Sanchez, *1 Peter for You* (Purcellville, VA: Good Book Company, 2016), chap. 9, "The Pathway to Glory."

is to purify his church by exposing false believers. For genuine Christians, the "fiery trial" (4:12) is meant to test the "genuineness of your faith" (1:7) and result "in praise and glory and honor at the revelation of Jesus Christ" (1:7). But this same "fiery trial" serves to separate the goats (unbelievers) from the sheep of God's flock.

1 Peter 5:1–4. In God's kindness, we don't have to persevere alone. God promised Israel that after the exile he would search for his sheep, gather them to himself, and shepherd them through a faithful shepherd from David's line on the basis of a new covenant (Isa. 40:9–11; Ezek. 34:11–31). As God's new-covenant people, we are God's sheep, he has gathered us, and Jesus is our shepherd (1 Pet. 5:4). Jesus, the chief shepherd from David's line, now guides his sheep through faithful human shepherds who are called to lead, protect, and provide for God's flock among them (5:1–4). In turn, God's sheep are to follow their leaders (5:5), humble themselves before God (5:6), and cast all their anxieties on him, because he cares for them (5:7). God has always cared for his people, and he will sustain us and guard us until he brings us all the way home from exile on this earth (1:5), and we obtain the outcome of our faith, the salvation of our souls (1:9).

Conclusion

When my wife, Jeanine, was pregnant with our fifth child, we took a trip to New York City. We hadn't settled on a baby name yet. While in the city, we went into a bookstore, and I found a baby-name book. Instead of starting at the beginning, I thumbed to the back and started reading. I came upon the name Zoe, which is Greek for "life." I loved it! Our Zoe was born on September 12, 2000. She is seventeen years old now, and she has more than lived up to her name. I often joke with her, saying that had I known how much she would grow to reflect her name, I would have named her Irene instead, because it is Greek for "peace."

I once heard someone say that "words mean stuff." Well, I would argue that words are usually pretty vague until they are in a context. When we chose the name Zoe, it was just a pretty name with a "cool" meaning. Now, however, in the context of her life, we realize just what "Zoe" means. It's the same with the words of the Bible. Isolated, they mean very little. It's not until we understand the context in which those words are used that we can truly understand what they mean. In this chapter I have tried to show what Peter's words mean by looking at the Old Testament context that Peter uses as a background for his message in 1 Peter. I have sought to keep the use of commentaries to a minimum to help you see that simply by working in God's Word, both the Old and New Testaments, you too may gain a better understanding of the message of Scripture.[14]

So next time you read a New Testament book, think of those Old Testament references as hyperlinks—you know, those links that are usually highlighted as you're reading an online blogpost or article.[15] Those links are there to help you gain a better understanding of what you're reading. Sometimes they only offer a simple definition, but at other times, they point you to a background article that helps you understand more about the topic you're reading. As you read 1 Peter, or any other book in the New Testament, click on that Old Testament "hyperlink" and see what it's all about. I promise that as you learn more about the context of the words you're reading, the Holy Spirit will bring greater illumination to your study. So, come! Enjoy! Taste and see that the Lord is good!

---

[14] I could not get into the details on how to interpret the Bible in this brief chapter. For a helpful introduction to biblical interpretation for teaching/preaching, I recommend David Helm, *Expositional Preaching: How We Speak God's Word Today* (Wheaton, IL: Crossway, 2014). In addition, the Charles Simeon Trust (http://simeontrust.org) offers training workshops for women on how to read, study, and teach the Bible to other women.

[15] I am thankful to Steve Timmis for the illustration of Old Testament quotations in the New Testament as "hyperlinks."

1

Born Again to a Living Hope

1 Peter 1:1–12

Kathleen Nielson

Let's start out by affirming that it is God's Word, God's breathed-out revelation of himself, we're dealing with in this volume. You'll hear a variety of voices in these chapters, but each is the voice of one who knows the truth of those words Peter quotes at the end of chapter 1:

> All flesh is like grass
>> and all its glory like the flower of grass.
> The grass withers,
>> and the flower falls,
> but the word of the Lord remains forever. (1 Pet. 1:24–25)

This is why we lean in to listen to the Scriptures: we are flowers that fall, and we need a word that doesn't. Like every human being, we need this eternal Word breathed out to us by the Lord of the universe. This Word is the good news received by grace through faith in the Lord Jesus Christ who died, who rose from the dead, and who is coming again soon.

This is good news indeed—but the biblical book we're expounding has rather a *sober* theme. The conference in which these talks were originally given was titled "Resurrection Life in a World of Suffering." It's clear to all of us these days that we must be sober about what kind of world we're living in. It is a world full of suffering—and for Christians, even distinct kinds of suffering. If you are reading this and you are not in the midst of suffering personally right now, praise God! But you almost certainly will suffer, and so will the generations of believers coming after you. And of course we must think of the brothers and sisters with whom we share this world and who suffer right now in all sorts of ways.

We do well to look suffering in the face and learn how to talk about it biblically. We come to God's Word not to forget about suffering for a little while; we come because we know that the good news we believe speaks right into the suffering, with the greatest hope. How does that happen? How is it that we believers can be at the same time the most unabashedly joyful and the most painfully sober people on the planet? The book of 1 Peter helps us with this question. Peter helps us grasp the hope of resurrection life in a world of suffering.

We begin with a big, weighty chunk of Scripture. In the first twelve verses that open his epistle Peter is purposefully doing something big. He's giving a panoramic view of the landscape before zooming in more closely. Peter begins by setting forth a big perspective of gospel hope. He wastes no time; we are not led gently into his letter. He does not prepare us for this panoramic view. He just lays it out there for us—and it might take our breath away! Just in the first two lines we encounter election, dispersion, foreknowledge, and sanctification. This first section indeed sets forth *a big perspective of gospel hope.*

Seeing the shape of this passage helps us take in the bigness. The gospel hope Peter will unfold is based on two main truths for believers in Jesus Christ: first, who we are in God's eyes (vv. 1–2), and, second, where we are in God's story (vv. 3–12). These truths are like our spiritual name and address, our identification that we must carry with us at all times. We need these truths to identify ourselves and to find our way home. Without these truths we won't grasp the hope of resurrection life. The suffering might threaten to overwhelm us. But Peter opens his book by pulling us up to get this big perspective, with these two truths shining out—and shining their light over the whole rest of the book.

I. Who We Are in God's Eyes (1:1–2)

Identities in Biblical Context

Peter, an apostle of Jesus Christ,

To those who are elect exiles of the Dispersion in Pontus, Galatia, Cappadocia, Asia, and Bithynia, according to the foreknowledge of God the Father, in the sanctification of the Spirit, for obedience to Jesus Christ and for sprinkling with his blood:

May grace and peace be multiplied to you. (1:1–2)

To get identity straight feels natural at the start of an epistle, because that's what you do at the start of any letter: you identify who's writing, and to whom you're writing. It's actually lovely that we get to grapple with this sober subject of suffering through a personal letter. A letter is different and often more comforting than, for example, a theological treatise on suffering, which, if you're right in the thick of suffering, you might not be able to digest. But a personal voice from a brother in the faith right to you—that's different.

Of course this letter isn't from just any brother. Peter identifies himself right at the start, in verse 1: "Peter, an apostle of Jesus Christ." His identification is simple and straightforward and carries a weight of authority that the early church clearly understood. An apostle was one who had been with Jesus and who had the authority to teach his truth. Peter was one of the disciples called out by Jesus, close to Jesus, loved by Jesus, severely rebuked by Jesus, and even failing miserably to follow Jesus—but finally forgiven, restored, and personally commissioned by Jesus, sent out to feed his sheep (cf. John 21:15–17).

In this epistle Peter is doing some substantive feeding of some really needy sheep. Most scholars believe Peter wrote this letter from Rome during the reign of the Roman emperor Nero, probably just a few years before the dramatic persecution of Christians that would take place under that same emperor. Peter himself would be martyred in those persecutions. But in this letter there's the sense of persecution *threatening*, arising on all sides, about to erupt.

What was the identity of those to whom Peter wrote? Verse 1 locates Peter's audience in "Pontus, Galatia, Cappadocia, Asia, and Bithynia." These place names all refer to Roman provinces in Asia Minor, which is now modern-day Turkey; many think the provinces are listed in the order of places along the route the letter would have been delivered. Mentioning Turkey actually should make us stop and consider how many centuries Christians have lived in that part of the world *and* endured persecution in that part of the world.

Peter names these believers with three weighty words: "*elect exiles* of the *Dispersion*." Each of these words is bursting with Old Testament history. The noun *exiles* first makes us think back to Israel and Judah being conquered and carried away into exile, first by the Assyrians and finally by the Babylonians. God's people were dispersed or spread out in lands not their own. That was called the "Jewish *diaspora*"—and so here we have "exiles of the *Dispersion*." But this raises a question: Is Peter here referring literally to exiled and dispersed Jews? Is he addressing only Jewish people in this letter? Probably not.

The context of the whole New Testament helps us here, with its various references to God's people as exiles. Hebrews 11, for example, sets up sort of an Old Testament "Hall of Faith" filled with exiles: Abraham, for example, sent out from his own country not knowing where he was going; or Moses, wandering in the wilderness. All these, Hebrews 11:13 says, "died in faith, not having received the things promised, but having seen them and greeted them from afar, and having acknowledged that they were strangers and *exiles* on the earth." They were looking for "a better country, that is, a heavenly one" (Heb. 11:16). God's people were often physical exiles, far from their land, but the main point seems to be that they were *spiritual* exiles, longing for their true land in heaven.

The Bible shows exile as a continuing picture of the life of faith. Exile works as a metaphor, a picture of God's people as citizens of heaven and not completely at home in the societies where we live. It makes sense, then, that Peter is writing not just to Jews but to Gentiles, or non-Jews, as well. He's addressing all God's people who lived in these Roman provinces but who had by faith become citizens of heaven. The churches in those areas actually included *many* Gentiles; he's probably referring to these Gentiles later in this chapter (vv. 14, 18) when he talks about their "former ignorance" and "the futile ways inherited from [their] forefathers." They hadn't been raised knowing about the one true God.

But let's not forget that adjective *elect* ("elect exiles of the Dispersion")—because that word *elect* means "chosen," and everybody knew that God's "chosen people" were the Jews. But Peter is speaking now to people of all nations who follow Jesus, and they are all elected, or chosen by God from the beginning. How incredibly comforting and clarifying that must have been to the believers from different backgrounds who were coming to faith through the missionary efforts of those early disciples! They were now part of a stream of God's chosen people, all sharing this experience of heading for a heavenly country and so not being fully at home in their earthly one.

Peter clinches this picture at the very end of the book, as he addresses these scattered believers: "She who is at Babylon, who is likewise chosen, sends you greetings" (5:13). Writing probably from Rome, Peter pictures Rome here as Babylon—Babylon being the historical enemy of God's people who took them into exile. In the New Testament, Babylon becomes a symbol of opposition to God's people, all the way through to the book of Revelation. So "she who is at Babylon" is symbolic code for "the church in Rome," who sends greetings to these other churches dispersed throughout the Roman Empire. And they're *all* chosen by God. They're all elect exiles.

Do you feel this letter from Peter reaching out to you? This picture language of believers as exiles stretches out to include *us*, now, as followers of Jesus; we are all elect exiles. We also join this centuries-long stream of God's people scattered throughout the nations, carrying deep in us the longing for our true home. It feels like the deepest kind of homesickness. The world would tell us to snuff out this longing by making ourselves at home here. But Peter helps us *name* that longing—and actually see it as part of our identity. Do you think of being an exile as part of your identity?

So many of you readers could tell about this experience of exile, in your various contexts. Some of you are teachers or administrators; that's a context where Christians sometimes feel a bit like foreigners these days. Educators who are Christ followers learn to tread with care and love and often great tension in order to live out their faith: managing curricula, dealing with rules and regulations, discerning when and how to give witness to the Lord Jesus. The needs are much deeper than dealing with mixed-gender bathrooms; we're traveling a road far from home—where we'll meet so many who are lost and who need help finding the way home.

Or there's the experience of students. What about those who experience same-sex attraction and who have chosen to live celibate lifestyles because they believe that's what Christ calls them to do? What about any young people who believe the Bible teaches God's design of marriage to be for one man and one woman? They all know certain kinds of exile, especially on university campuses.

What about family contexts? I think of a young husband and wife who are called to take the gospel to another country but whose parents are up in arms against their children's throwing away all the time and money invested in a good education that should be getting them good jobs with salaries, right close to home. They're exiled at home.

How about contexts farther away? My husband and I regularly spend time in Indonesia; I'm thinking of a number of young Indonesian teachers at Christian schools in that country, and picturing their faces around dinner tables telling about their conversion or their families' conversion to Christianity. Some of them are cut off now from familiar contexts and homes, and some of them still hail from areas where Christians are not welcome. In one way or another many of them are exiles, and they are some of the most joyful exiles I've ever met. And we must keep looking farther, of course, to take in the growing numbers in our world who are exiles in every sense of the word—the hundreds of thousands of Christians who have fled Iraq and Syria, for example. Oh, how much we have to learn about exile, about suffering as aliens in one place while our true citizenship lies in another.

Identities Defined by God

But let's go on: this opening sentence is not finished! In verse 2 Peter adds three phrases that describe these elect exiles. We mustn't miss this, because it is so beautiful. Look at the three phrases in verse 2 and see there the three persons of the Godhead together defining what it means to be an elect exile. You don't get to define exile by yourself. We could all write our own descriptions of what it feels like to be an exile. But here's God's definition, in terms of himself. This is what an exile looks like from God's eyes. Oh, if we could see it this way—and see ourselves this way.

First, as believers we are elect exiles *according to the foreknowledge of God the Father* (v. 2). Peter is following up on "elect" here, explaining God's sovereign choice in terms of his "foreknowledge."

This word "foreknowledge" expresses a kind of knowing that is so personal and powerful it can also be used for God's foreknowing of Jesus, who was "foreknown before the foundation of the world" (v. 20). If you are a believer, God has known you that deeply forever. We do not have to create our own identity; we are known. Eternally known. Our placing in this world as we are is no random swirl of the universe. Your hearing the gospel is no accident. Peter is telling you as a believer that God sovereignly planned for you to be a citizen of heaven—and for you to long for heaven. He even planned for you to wander in whatever hard place you're wandering and feeling like an exile for a little while; this is all according to the foreknowledge of God the Father. Peter helps us experience our exile not as lost orphans but rather as chosen children heading home.

Second, continuing in verse 2, we are elect exiles *in the sanctification of the Spirit*. This means we've been set apart as God's holy people through the work of his Holy Spirit. Again, we cannot make this happen ourselves. Now, sanctification often refers to the whole process of becoming holy and conformed to the image of Christ, but it can also refer to the initial setting apart as holy that happens when the Spirit brings new life to a dead soul—what Paul calls "the washing of regeneration and renewal of the Holy Spirit" (Titus 3:5). It's through this initial work of the Holy Spirit that we actually become exiles. Set apart for God, we have a new citizenship, and we're given a new inheritance in heaven. Our whole relationship to this world is changed.

We have a *who*, a *how*, and a *why* here. *Who* determines that we'll be elect exiles? God the Father. *How* do we become elect exiles? Through the Spirit. And, finally, *why* do we become elect exiles? The third phrase in verse 2 has two matching parts to it, and they're both all about Jesus: "for obedience to Jesus Christ and for sprinkling with his blood." Why are we made exiles? To obey the Lord Jesus.

But what's this "sprinkling with his blood"? Let's put obedience together with the blood here. Peter is connecting again to the

Old Testament, most likely to a scene in Exodus 24:1–8, where, after the exodus from Egypt, all the Israelites gather at Mount Sinai. It's an awesome scene. The mountain shakes. Moses builds a huge altar and offers sacrifices, and there are basins full of oxen blood. Half the blood is thrown against the altar and the other half on the people as Moses reads the words from the Lord and the people vow to obey. In that scene the Lord covenants with his people, and they are made the people of God.

But those to whom Peter writes had been made the people of God through a *new* covenant, the covenant in Christ's blood. First Peter 1:18–19 tells us they were ransomed "not with perishable things such as silver or gold, but with the precious blood of Christ, like that of a lamb without blemish or spot." Their obedience to Jesus Christ is first and foremost the obedience of faith in that blood. Of course obedience is a lifelong call, but here's the starting point: in the blood of Christ that redeems us. All the obedience Peter's going to call for in this book is the obedience of those who *have been made holy* by the death of Christ on their behalf—sprinkled with his blood.

Let's put this all together. What's our identity as believers? It's that of elect exiles—elect exiles sovereignly foreknown by the Father, elect exiles sanctified by the Spirit, elect exiles called to obey the Lord Jesus who shed his blood for us. Is this how you see yourself? Do you picture the Godhead all around you and at work for you and in you and through you—Father, Son, and Holy Spirit? Our identity as elect exiles doesn't lose its pain and suffering, but our exile is lighted up with hope when we see it as God shows it to us here. From this big perspective, what do we see? We see *him*. This epistle will ask us to see our exile lighted up by God himself, as he leans down all around us to save us. What a picture of grace! With this identity we can find grace and peace multiplied, even as Peter prays for his readers there at the end of verse 2: "May grace and peace be multiplied to you." (We'll come back to that.)

Now, you've surely noticed that we've already spent half of this chapter on just two verses! We'll accelerate. But those first couple of verses are crucial; they set us up to take in the whole book from this big perspective of gospel hope as we see first this truth of who we are in God's eyes. Now we're ready to move on.

II. Where We Are in God's Story (1:3–12)

Looking to the Future

> Blessed be the God and Father of our Lord Jesus Christ! According to his great mercy, he has caused us to be born again to a living hope through the resurrection of Jesus Christ from the dead, to an inheritance that is imperishable, undefiled, and unfading, kept in heaven for you, who by God's power are being guarded through faith for a salvation ready to be revealed in the last time. (1:3–5)

The whole second section (vv. 3–12) locates us in God's story—but let's notice that Peter does not take us through the story chronologically. He does not move from past to present to future. You might say he goes backward. He *starts* with the future. God can do that; he's the God who elects and foreknows. God can think future-first, and he's asking us here to think that way too.

Verses 3–5 burst out in praise to God for our future hope. The opening in verse 3 sounds a lot like the traditional Jewish prayers that would begin with words such as, "Blessed be the Lord, the God of Israel." Only here, Peter changes it: "Blessed be the God and Father of our Lord Jesus Christ!" This prayer is focused on Christ, and specifically on the *resurrected* Christ, the source of all hope. It's God the Father of the Lord Jesus who is praised here, for mercifully and sovereignly causing us to be born again to a living hope. How? Through the resurrection of Jesus Christ from the dead. Isn't it interesting that Peter doesn't say "through the death and resurrection of Jesus Christ"—even though, of course, that is true. Peter is focusing on the far side of salvation here, on the resurrection that stretches the hope of our salvation eternally into the future. We are alive now in the risen Christ, *and*, because Christ rose from the dead, so will we. That is our certain hope.

We're not talking here about the sort of hope we often speak of, as in, "I hope that person will like me," or, "I hope this pill works," or, "I hope we'll have enough money to pay our bills this month." We live with so many little and big hopes that are uncertain, and yet we keep hoping. So often our hopes are disappointed.

But in order to live we need hope, real hope, as much as we need food and rest. James Stockdale, the highest-ranked naval officer ever imprisoned in North Vietnam, famously explored the necessity of hope during his eight years of torture-filled captivity, from 1965 to 1973. He learned that sentimental or unfounded hope won't work. When asked later which prisoners didn't make it, Stockdale said:

> Oh, that's easy. The optimists. They were the ones who said, "We're going to be out by Christmas." And Christmas would come, and Christmas would go. Then they'd say, "We're going to be out by Easter." And Easter would come, and Easter would go. And then Thanksgiving, and then it would be Christmas again. And they died of a broken heart.[1]

Stockdale lived out what's become known as the Stockdale Paradox: on the one hand, there must be a facing of brutal present reality (for him it was the reality of chains and torture that might last a long time), but, on the other hand, there must be strong, solid hope in a finally good end. People can't live without hope. Stockdale said, "I never doubted not only that I would get out but also that I would prevail in the end and turn the experience into the defining event of my life, which, in retrospect, I would not trade."[2]

---

[1] In his best seller, *Good to Great: Why Some Companies Make the Leap . . . and Others Don't* (New York: HarperCollins, 2001), Jim Collins reports on a personal interview with Admiral Jim Stockdale (pp. 83–37). Collins uses Stockdale's example to show that one huge factor in a company's success is the way in which its leaders respond to difficult challenges.
[2] Ibid.

Stockdale was on to something far beyond his own story, which thankfully unfolded to bring his release from prison. According to the Scriptures, in the end there's only one sure hope, because the life-and-death outcome of that hope has been proven. Jesus Christ died on that cross, bearing our sins, and he rose from the dead, sealing our salvation and our hope. Our living hope isn't some abstract feeling; our living hope is Jesus himself.

Are you a person of hope? On what is your hope based? These verses unfold the substance of this living hope by calling it "an inheritance that is imperishable, undefiled, and unfading" (v. 4). "Inheritance" is another word ringing with Old Testament meaning, for the Jews were indeed given an inheritance by God: a land. The only problem was that that inheritance of land *did* become defiled. By drought, and enemies' devastation, and foreign domination. By sin, finally. In contrast, however, Peter is telling these elect exiles that in the living Christ they have an inheritance that won't ever tarnish or perish. It's nothing like treasures on earth where moth and rust destroy and where thieves break in and steal. In fact, this isn't treasure you lay up, but rather inheritance that is given to you and "kept in heaven for you."

That phrase should make us take a deep breath. God is keeping this inheritance for us. We spend our lives trying to keep things. To keep things safe. To keep things from being spoiled. And not just things such as money and houses and clothes and food—all that is hard enough. But *people*: we try to keep children safe and sound, our elderly parents, our own bodies. Oh, how hard we work to keep our bodies from fading, from being defiled by people who would harm us, ultimately from perishing. We spend a lot of energy trying to keep many things. Ultimately, we can't. But here's the hope: this inheritance of life forever with Jesus is kept in heaven for us. And God is the perfect keeper. His inheritance to us in Christ will never perish or be defiled or fade.

Now, some of you might not be connecting meaningfully with this inheritance in heaven, because the reality of your earthly life right now is pretty consuming and just downright hard. Peter knew you were going to feel like that! And so he does something wonderful with the next phrases in this sentence: he winds them right back around to you—you "who by God's power are being guarded through faith for a salvation ready to be revealed in the last time" (v. 5). So, not only is this inheritance kept for us, but God is keeping us for this inheritance! We're under guard, verse 5 says, by God's power first and foremost, *and* through faith, as we trust in that power.

What we're being kept for is not far away; it's imminent: "ready to be revealed in the last time." It's *ready*! It's coming. We're about to see it, and it's right there. Or, more accurately, we're about to see *him*, and he is right there—Jesus is right there, ready to appear! We're seeing here why Peter starts with the future, as he tells where we are in God's story. The story is in motion toward this inheritance, this living Lord Jesus, and so indeed we live as people born again to a living hope.

Rejoicing in the Present

In this you rejoice, though now for a little while, if necessary, you have been grieved by various trials, so that the tested genuineness of your faith—more precious than gold that perishes though it is tested by fire—may be found to result in praise and glory and honor at the revelation of Jesus Christ. Though you have not seen him, you love him. Though you do not now see him, you believe in him and rejoice with joy that is inexpressible and filled with glory, obtaining the outcome of your faith, the salvation of your souls. (1:6–9)

As he positions us future-facing in God's story, Peter doesn't ignore the present. He's showing what Stockdale's Paradox gets at: we must confront the reality of *now*, even as we hope. When he says, "In this you rejoice," the word "this" refers to the whole future hope he's just laid out. But the word "rejoice" brings a very present reality. There's a "now" focus to this section: "though *now* for a little while, if necessary, you have been grieved by various trials" (v. 6) and, "Though you do not *now* see him" (v. 8b). Verses 6–9 speak to right now, and they include the most amazing combination of joy and grief. That's a deep word in verse 6: "grieved." It's not just a little sadness. It's deep sorrow. By *various* trials, Peter says. It's true that Peter will focus on the distinct trials suffered by believers who are scorned or persecuted, but here at the start there seems to be a compassionate wideness in Peter's grasp of all our various trials during this little while.

How long do you think is "a little while"? What kind of time are we talking about? Probably God's time, don't you think? It's most likely not just a few days or weeks. It's probably not just a brief part of our exile; it's more likely the whole thing—because this whole little while, in light of eternity, is just like a breath. A vapor.

And so for a little while we lose loved ones; we are lonely or deserted; we are sick; we are poor; we cry; we bleed; we are oppressed or mistreated by those around us. Some of you are right in the midst of it—and not one of us is free while some of us are suffering. That means the whole body of Christ is suffering for this little while, until he returns.

But what about the rejoicing? The wonder is that the rejoicing isn't in the future; it's in the present. Right now, for a little while, we rejoice and we grieve. How is that possible? I don't know. But I've *seen* it; haven't you? I've felt it; haven't you? I felt it not long ago in the presence of my father as he went home to heaven. Heaven was obviously right there, and my father from his bed raised his arm like he'd been called on, took a few last breaths, and entered it. I so intensely wanted to see what he was seeing as he kind of leaned forward; it was right there. The Lord was right there. Just a few hours earlier I had read out loud to Dad these verses we're studying. My father was a pastor, and he was always interested in whatever passage I was working on. So we had just heard these words about this living hope, this inheritance kept in heaven for us—and Dad just went on and claimed it. And my mother and I grieved deeply. And we rejoiced deeply.

Upon the death of Helen Roseveare in 2016, I read again about this remarkable woman who served as a missionary doctor in the Congo in the mid-twentieth century. Just a few years ago I had the privilege of talking with Dr. Roseveare at a women's conference in Belfast, Northern Ireland—and a stronger, more shining saint of an older woman you could never hope to meet. I was so moved to read again the story of how Helen came to know the Lord during her Cambridge University years. She excelled in medical school and then headed right off to Africa, where she labored for decades building hospitals and training medical workers and teaching the Bible. Through it all she struggled like we all do with her own longings and pride and stubborn self; she grew up in the Lord through every challenging experience he sent her way. She has spoken and written with great honesty about her life; Helen Roseveare is one of those women whose stories it is good for us to hear.

In 1964, during political uprisings in the Congo, Helen's house was raided by rebels, and she and others were captured and eventually held prisoner for several months. When she tried at first to escape, she was brutally treated: she was beaten, her teeth were knocked out, and she was raped. Here's a bit of what she said later about that horrific experience:

> I wasn't praying. I was beyond praying. Someone back home was praying earnestly for me. If I'd prayed any prayer it would have been, "My God, my God why hast thou forsaken me?" And suddenly, there was God. I didn't see a vision, I didn't hear a voice, I just knew with every ounce of my being that God was actually, vitally there. God in all his majesty and power. He stretched out his arms to me. He surrounded me with his love.[3]

---

[3] Helen Roseveare's story can be found through a number of sources, including YouTube live interviews. She authored an autobiography titled *Give Me This Mountain* (London: Inter-Varsity

As she recounted this story, Helen Roseveare clearly and simply turned her listeners to Jesus:

> Fantastic, the privilege of being identified with our Savior.
> . . . One word became unbelievably clear, and that word was
> privilege. [God] didn't take away pain or cruelty or humilia-
> tion. No! It was all there, but now it was altogether different.
> It was with him, for him, in him. He was actually offering me
> the inestimable privilege of sharing in some little way the edge
> of the fellowship of his suffering.

It seems almost inconceivable to us to hear these words. And yet they ring true. Some even more contemporary stories of Christians who suffer with grace and joy can be found in Mindy Belz's *They Say We Are Infidels: On the Run from ISIS with Persecuted Christians in the Middle East.*[4] How can we teach the next generation this strange, wonderful mix of joy and grief? We need to teach it, don't we? We all need to learn and to teach that this little while of sojourn on this earth is not for the purpose of ease and prosperity but that with the joy will come all kinds of trials, in which we can rejoice as those sustained by gospel hope.

What sustains us is further unfolded in verse 7: the prospect that the tested genuineness of our faith—more precious than gold that perishes though it is tested by fire—may be found to result in praise and glory and honor at the revelation of Jesus Christ, when he comes again. Our faith that's gone through the fire is that "precious" to our Lord. Your faith is not just yours; it is God's gift to you, and he knows how much it cost. He *values* it. But to whom will the resulting honor be given? Certainly to our Savior. But perhaps to us as well—although the glory will all be his, shining in us.

Fellowship, 1966). The quotations here are taken from her address to the Urbana gathering of 1976, reported by Jack Voelkel on the urbana.com website in a blog titled "Helen Roseveare: Courageous Doctor in the Congo," February 18, 2007, accessed April 19, 2017, https://urbana.org /blog/helen-roseveare. Noël Piper gives a good summary account of Roseveare's ministry in *Faithful Women and their Extraordinary God* (Wheaton, IL: Crossway, 2005).

[4] Mindy Belz, *They Say We Are Infidels: On the Run from ISIS with Persecuted Christians in the Middle East* (Carol Stream, IL: Tyndale, 2016).

And so we begin to understand that little phrase "if necessary" there in verse 6. Why might it be necessary for us to be grieved by various trials?

> When through fiery trials thy pathway shall lie,
> My grace, all sufficient, shall be thy supply;
> The flame shall not hurt thee; *I only design*
> Thy dross to consume, and thy gold to refine.[5]

Let's say it right out and wonder at it: suffering is actually part of God's plan (and so necessary) to bring about the shining riches of praise and glory and honor. Glory is the shining forth of God's very being. His glory is what he's after, shining forth even in us! Gold can't begin to picture it. Of course we cannot understand this glory without beginning at the cross, with the suffering of our Savior on our behalf. There was glory revealed. As we trust our Savior and then follow after him, what the apostle Paul says is true: our present sufferings are not worth comparing with the glory that is to be revealed in us (Rom. 8:18)—an eternal weight of glory (2 Cor. 4:17).

What is it that makes us long for this glory? Do you long for it? What makes us go through the fire? I think the answer comes in that next marvelous verse 8. And the answer is Jesus himself. Not the idea of Jesus, or the truth about him, but the Lord Jesus himself. The risen one, there at the hand of God shining in glory— right now, right there. Don't you long to see him? Peter got to see him on earth, looked into his face and heard his voice. Peter saw him die, saw him resurrected, saw him standing there, asking, "Peter, do you love me?" We cannot yet share that experience of looking into Jesus's face—not yet. But right now by faith we can read these words and believe them: "Though you have not seen him, you love him. Though you do not *now* see him, you believe in him and rejoice with joy" (v. 8). Here's the rejoicing that bookends

---

[5] From the text of the hymn "How Firm a Foundation," attributed to Robert Keen, ca. 1787; emphasis added.

this little section (cf. v. 6). It's a rejoicing filled with the glory of the Savior we love.

Did you hear what happened to glory in those verses? It jumped into the present. Peter is saying not only that glory will be the result of our testing, but also that our joy right now is filled with glory. That's because we know and love the glorified Lord Jesus. Right now. Even not yet seeing him. We begin to shine like him.

Trusting in What's Past

Concerning this salvation, the prophets who prophesied about the grace that was to be yours searched and inquired carefully, inquiring what person or time the Spirit of Christ in them was indicating when he predicted the sufferings of Christ and the subsequent glories. It was revealed to them that they were serving not themselves but you, in the things that have now been announced to you through those who preached the good news to you by the Holy Spirit sent from heaven, things into which angels long to look. (1:10–12)

To clarify our present love for Jesus, Peter looks to the past, in verses 10–12. We need to get the whole story. For the whole story has always been pointing toward Jesus, specifically toward his *suffering* and his *glory*. Peter makes clear that the Spirit of Christ was leading the Old Testament prophets who searched and inquired so carefully—and they were inquiring specifically concerning the person and time of "the sufferings of Christ and the subsequent glories" (v. 11). There's the pattern—suffering and glory—laid down in the past in God's Word, and pointing to Jesus, who would come and fulfill this Word.

Peter is telling us that we can know Jesus by seeing him in all the Scriptures from the beginning. According to Peter's prophetic word, the Scriptures have always been inspired by the Spirit of Christ and have been revealing Christ—his suffering and his glory. Peter wants us to know how privileged we are to be given the full story of salvation now revealed in Christ, what he calls "the grace that was to be yours" (v. 10). These truths of grace are so wonderful that angels long to look into them, and *we* actually have them delivered to us, preached to us with their meaning uncovered. What amazing grace! Just as Juan Sanchez makes clear in his introductory chapter, the way Peter teaches in this epistle is to refer constantly to Old Testament writings and to show how they reveal Jesus. Of course Peter learned this from the master—from Jesus himself.

If you're just not quite sure yet what to do with all this stuff about suffering and testing by fire and aiming for glory, do this one thing: keep filling yourself with all of Scripture's inspired words from God. They will show his Son to you. They will teach you about suffering and glory, because they will teach you about Jesus. If you don't yet know Jesus personally, if you have not come to faith in him as the Lord who died for you and who lives for you, I pray you will be drawn to him by these words, as the Spirit draws you. I pray that all of us would be drawn by these opening words of Peter to read on—and to love and follow Jesus.

Now That We've Got the Big Picture

We've watched Peter in these opening verses lay out a big perspective of gospel hope by showing believers who we are in God's eyes and where we are in God's story. We're *named* and we're *placed* by God himself. This is revolutionary, to see our identity as God's people from God's eyes. This is a perspective of hope—living hope. Peter's blessing is the best response: "Blessed be the God and Father of our Lord Jesus Christ!" (v. 3).

Let's ask one final question: What does Peter aim for us to do with these truths that he lays out here and that he will unfold through the rest of the book? Peter actually tells us what he's after in this book. It doesn't come until the end, and we'll understand it better when we come to it, but it's good to bear it in mind from the start. In the final chapter Peter says this: "I have written briefly to you, exhorting and declaring that this is the true grace of God.

Stand firm in it" (5:12). There it is. Peter stands back at the end and says that what he's really after is that these believers would stand firm in the grace of God. We heard grace at the beginning: "May grace and peace be multiplied to you" (1:2). From beginning to end this epistle points us to the grace of God in causing us to be born again to a living hope, in Christ Jesus our Lord.

This is what Peter wants us to stand firm *in*: God's grace to us in Christ. Even in a world of suffering, we can sing: *When through fiery trials thy pathway shall lie, my grace all sufficient shall be thy supply*. The very next passage will tell us what kind of action grows from this grace. But first we had to get the big picture clear, this picture framed in grace. It's grace that we get to know our spiritual name and address—and we need to carry this identification with us always, because with this identification we can get home. As followers of Jesus, we're far from our true country where we long to be. But Peter sets forth this big perspective of gospel hope that lights up the landscape all around us so that we can see ourselves as elect exiles born again to a living hope—and heading home.

Reflect and Pray

Reflect on each question and then take a moment to speak or write the prayers that grow from those reflections.

1. Read again through the first couple verses of 1 Peter and think about that description of believers as "elect exiles." How do these verses help us understand what this description means? In what ways do you as a Christian identify personally with this description?

2. This chapter pointed out the centrality of *future hope* in the biblical text. What several phrases from 1 Peter 1:1–12 stand out to you as defining our future hope? How should this hope affect our prayers for ourselves and for those around us in our families, our churches, and our world?

3. What various truths about *suffering* do we find in this introductory passage to 1 Peter? How do these verses set suffering in a certain perspective? What tends to be your perspective on suffering, and how do you think 1 Peter might affect that perspective?

Think Like an Expositor: Comments from Kathleen Nielson

1. On the process of preparing to teach 1 Peter 1:1–12:

It was great to have over a year of knowing that this passage was coming up. I had never taught these verses specifically before, although I had studied the book in a Bible study—so I read and reread the whole book, praying through it, and marking repeated words and themes. I memorized verses 3–9 so that I could think on them freely, and printed out my passage to mark up and muse over. I came to love it and to love worshiping through it, but I also became a little intimidated by its density—when you're faced with election, foreknowledge, sanctification, obedience, and blood sprinkling in the first two verses, you know you're facing something much bigger than you.

And that turned out to be the wonderful point: this is a big introduction that establishes a big perspective of gospel hope that shines through this whole letter of encouragement to those who are suffering and need this hope. My main concern was to find a way to talk about this big gospel hope in a manner that would be clear and faithful to the text.

2. On the challenge of teaching an opening passage to a book:

You want to do so much when you're teaching the first verses of a book. You want to set up the historical context, and you want to get at the main theme, and so forth. But God's Word always does the work for us: in digging into verse 1, for example, we're led naturally to bring in the writer and audience and historical context of this letter. The most helpful process for me was simply to try to be obedient to the structure of the passage. There's a greeting (vv. 1–2) in which Peter defines not just historically but also theologically the identity of these believers to whom he's writing. And then there's a praise-filled section (vv. 3–12) that glories in our future hope through the resurrected Christ; our present rejoicing in Christ even through trials; and the past witness to Christ through the prophetic writings. It seemed faithful to the text to summarize this structure as presenting "who we are in God's eyes" (vv. 1–2) and "where we are in God's story" (vv. 3–12).

I loved beginning to uncover this structure. I was helped in the process by participating in a workshop on biblical exposition where we studied 1 Peter, and where in one small-group session we worked through this passage together and clarified especially the future/present/past flow of verses 3–12. And in God's providence, our church did a series on 1 Peter in the months before the conference, and I got to hear a sermon in my home congregation on my passage—what a gift. After individual and prayerful wrestling with the text, I'm always so grateful for the wisdom of the believers around me. What a joy to receive this Word as a part of God's people.

3. On one aspect of this text that especially moved and challenged you:

The real, true hope of this passage really seeped into my soul. The reality of the risen Christ and this inheritance that is kept in heaven for us seems like such a present reality to Peter as he writes, and it became a more present reality to me through studying these verses. What amazing words: "Though you have not seen him, you love him." I believe that our study should be worship, but of course at times it feels more grueling and less worshipful than at others! This passage was an easy and a marvelous one to worship through, and I'm thankful for that.

2

Living Resurrection Life

1 Peter 1:13–2:3

Jen Wilkin

On June 4, 1940, a man of average appearance rose to address the British House of Commons. He was an unlikely orator, having had to overcome both a lisp and a stammer in his boyhood. Nothing about his early life had indicated he would find himself here. His teachers had dubbed him careless, forgetful, and devoid of punctuality. He stood a mere 5 feet 6 inches in height. But on this day, in the full assurance of his authority to speak, and in the absolute conviction of the urgency of the moment, Winston Churchill took the floor. He delivered his now historic address, "We Shall Fight Them on the Beaches," a speech that both inspired and catalyzed, challenging the British people to redouble their resolve to fight the Nazi threat:

> We shall go on to the end, we shall fight in France, we shall
> fight on the seas and oceans, we shall fight with growing con-
> fidence and growing strength in the air, we shall defend our

Island, whatever the cost may be, we shall fight on the beaches, we shall fight on the landing grounds, we shall fight in the fields and in the streets, we shall fight in the hills; we shall never surrender . . . until, in God's good time, the New World, with all its power and might, steps forth to the rescue and the liberation of the old.[1]

I'm struck by the similarity between this speech and Peter's letter to five fledgling churches in Asia Minor. An unlikely messenger with a history of inadequacy in both speech and action, now risen to full authority, charges those beset with fear and loss to set their hope on future victory, exhorting them to unity, perseverance, and action.

In the first twelve verses of his epistle, Peter unfolds for his readers a picture of their glorious inheritance. It is an inheritance secured in the finished work of Christ, who acted at the will of the Father, through the power of the Spirit. It is kept safe for them. Though now they endure difficulty of all kinds on account of their faith, these trials are fleeting. They have been "born again," given good news to sustain them through whatever this brief life may throw at them—a good news so beautiful that the esteemed prophets of old searched diligently for it, and the holy angels of heaven longed to plumb its depths.

Having established the beauty and sufficiency of their inheritance, Peter charges his hearers to respond accordingly, following the pattern of Christ's faithful sufferings on the way to subsequent glories. He offers four admonitions: hope fully (1:13), be holy (1:14–16), fear rightly (1:17–21), and love earnestly (1:22–25). To fulfill all four of these admonitions, he prescribes a necessary diet for the newborn believers of Asia Minor: pure spiritual milk (2:2). As we move through 1 Peter 1:13–2:3, we witness Peter demonstrate tender care for his vulnerable readers, fledglings in

---

[1] "We Shall Fight on the Beaches," The International Churchill Society, April 13, 2017, accessed December 7, 2017, https:www.winstonchurchill.org/resources/speeches/1940-the-finest-hour/we-shall-fight-on-the-beaches/.

the faith weighed down by trial and beset by fear. Though they do not now see Christ in the flesh, Peter—the eyewitness to his life and ministry—encourages them to persevere for the refining of their faith and the joy of their salvation.

Hope Fully (1:13)

Therefore, preparing your minds for action, and being sober-minded, set your hope fully on the grace that will be brought to you at the revelation of Jesus Christ. (1:13)

Peter begins his exhortations with an important word: "Therefore." In light of your beautiful inheritance in Christ, what ought you to do? Set your hope fully on the grace that is to be brought to you at the revelation of Jesus Christ. A full revelation of Christ is coming, on the day of his return. Place your hope in that day, because this day may be filled with trial and sorrow. But how are you to do so? Peter specifies two ways: preparing your minds for action and being sober-minded.

The phrase "preparing your minds for action" can be translated literally as "girding up the loins of your mind." It is a reference to the practice of preparing for battle. The ancients wore long robes, which would have hampered their ability to fight. Before going into battle, they bound them up around their waists to allow for freedom of motion. Entering into combat while wearing clothing that restricted their movements would have been completely foolish. Peter indicates to his hearers that having a rightly placed hope requires more than good intentions. They must be ready to fight. The battle for holiness requires that they prepare themselves as a soldier prepares for war, letting nothing encumber their ability to fight.

Note also where this battle for holiness begins. It is the believer's mind that must be readied for war. When we strive to live lives of holiness, we often begin by attempting to curtail sinful behaviors: *I should swear less. I should stop spending impulsively.*

But Peter points us to the source of our sin: our thoughts. Every sinful action we engage in is the result of a sinful thought that fed a sinful desire. If we want to set our hope fully on grace, we must deal with our sin at the source.

Temptation presents itself to the mind as a reasonable choice. We allow our thoughts to dwell on its reasonableness, fueling our desires. And as James tells us, "Desire when it has conceived gives birth to sin, and sin when it is fully grown brings forth death" (James 1:15). For this reason, Paul admonishes us to seek transformation not through the renewing of our actions or our desires, but through the renewing of our minds (Rom. 12:2).

We see the progression from thought to desire to action all the time in our daily lives. I used to love milkshakes from my favorite fast-food restaurant. But one day, as I pulled up to the drive-through menu, I noticed what would be the beginning of the end of my love affair with them. The FDA had mandated that the nutritional content be noted next to every item on the menu. It turns out that my milkshake was killing me. Once my mind knew what was in it, my desire to have one began to diminish, and my menu choices began to change. So it is with sin. Understanding a sin's consequences helps break our desire to give in to it, resulting in a turning away from what once tempted us. Once we know sin is a killer, it doesn't look as sweet. Right thinking informs right desires, which lead to right actions. But thinking rightly will be a battle. We must be prepared to fight.

Peter also notes that setting our hope fully on Christ requires a second type of mental preparedness: sober-mindedness. The opposite of soberness is drunkenness. Think about what a drunk person is like. His perception is skewed so that he cannot think clearly, nor can he govern his desires or actions. He is a danger to himself and others, unpredictable and unreliable, unable to be swayed by wise counsel. By contrast, Peter urges his hearers to be self-controlled and single-minded as they live out their salvation.

If we are to set our hope fully on Christ, we must be fully attuned to the things of Christ with great seriousness.

It is interesting that Peter includes the word "fully" at all. Why not just tell us to set our hope on the grace that will be brought to us? Why "set our hope *fully* on grace?" Because it is possible, and indeed common, for the believer to function as one with a hope placed partially on grace and partially elsewhere. We are prone to placing our hope on our own good deeds, or on a spouse or our children, or on a pastor or president. We may place it on a bank account or a career, or even on the size of our social media accounts. We tell ourselves that we hope in Christ, but what we mean is that we hope in Christ and _____.

We are people of divided allegiances, divided hopes. We hedge our bets. We are the double-minded man of James 1:6–8, tossed about by waves of doubt. We are those Jesus warned about, storing up treasures both on earth and in heaven. Peter calls us instead to hope *fully* on grace, ready to battle doubt and temptation, soberly weighing the cost of divided loyalties. Those who place their hope fully on grace forgo the vain pleasures of this world and look to Christ. They treasure a future inheritance rather than seeking one in the present. Peter's original audience was facing the loss of social, financial, and familial stability as a result of their conversion. Their current situation left little room for hope by human standards. To them, Peter's call to a full hope in a future security would have been a mercy. It is for modern ears, as well. We also face uncertainty and loss in this life. But we do not place our hope in this life. Rather, we place it fully on the future grace that awaits us.

How are sober-mindedness and mental battle-readiness achieved and sustained? As we will see, they are gained by craving the Word.

Be Holy (1:14–16)

As obedient children, do not be conformed to the passions of your former ignorance, but as he who called you is holy, you also be holy in all your conduct, since it is written, "You shall be holy, for I am holy." (1:14–16)

Peter builds on his admonition to set our hope fully on grace by calling his hearers to be holy in all they do. He does so by appealing to a frequently repeated command in the Old Testament, one that Jewish converts in his audience would have recognized immediately. The command to be holy as God is holy is stated explicitly four times in Leviticus and is echoed in the words of Jesus in Matthew 5:48: "You therefore must be perfect, as your heavenly Father is perfect." It is difficult to imagine a more daunting command than this, yet both the Old Testament and New Testament call followers of the one true God to bear his image by living holy lives. The call to be holy is a call to be set apart, to live as the aliens and strangers Peter will call us to be in chapter 2. For what could be more noticeably strange than a life lived in devoted obedience to God?

In contrast to the children of obedience Peter charges us to be, the Bible calls those who reject the good news of the gospel the "sons of disobedience" (Eph. 2:2). Obedience to God's law is the hallmark of genuine faith. The gospel liberates us from condemnation under the law. Whereas once it was above us as a taskmaster, requiring what we could never fulfill, by grace the law has become for us the narrow path beneath our feet, guiding us in what is safe and right, and in what brings glory to God. No longer must we conform to the passions of our former ignorance. That ignorance is dispelled as our minds are renewed and our desires turn away from disobedience toward obedience. We begin to think, feel, act, and speak like Christ, who fulfilled the law. Christ was (and is) holy as his heavenly Father is holy. So ought we to strive to be, not to earn salvation, but as evidence that salvation has occurred.

As Peter's contemporary John notes, "For this is the love of God, that we keep his commandments. And his commandments are not burdensome" (1 John 5:3). Don't miss that. We show our love for God by obeying his commands. His commands are not burdensome to those who love him. The law, which was once a millstone, is no longer so. This is not to say that God's commands are not difficult. They are certainly difficult, as Peter's listeners know firsthand. Following them means the loss of comfort in this life: rejection by family and friends, persecution, ridicule, and hardship. It means being singled out as alien and strange. These are very real difficulties that require us to set our hope fully on grace. But obeying God's commands is not a burden that we resent or avoid. It is a joyful duty that we eagerly undertake out of gratitude for the lavish grace we have received.

Fear Rightly (1:17–21)

> And if you call on him as Father who judges impartially according to each one's deeds, conduct yourselves with fear throughout the time of your exile, knowing that you were ransomed from the futile ways inherited from your forefathers, not with perishable things such as silver or gold, but with the precious blood of Christ, like that of a lamb without blemish or spot. He was foreknown before the foundation of the world but was made manifest in the last times for the sake of you who through him are believers in God, who raised him from the dead and gave him glory, so that your faith and hope are in God. (1:17–21)

Peter's third admonition in light of our inheritance is that we conduct ourselves with fear. Simple enough. Just turn on the evening news and we find ourselves with ample fuel for fear. Peter's audience was no different. But fear of physical loss, financial ruin, or political turmoil is not what Peter has in view. Rather, he admonishes believers to fear God. We are to lead lives characterized by reverence toward our Father and judge.

Both the ideas of obedience and fear of God have fallen out of favor in many Christian circles. He is often celebrated as loving Father, but rarely as just judge. The God of our modern invention does not require obedience, nor does he require our reverence. He wants only our acceptance of his gracious invitation to relationship and our enjoyment of his love. He is a God who is near and approachable, but he has lost all traces of the transcendence ascribed to him in the Scriptures. Peter reminds his hearers that the God who has condescended to them through Christ is both a personal, loving Father and an impartial judge of the hearts of men (1:17). Such a God is worthy of not just our adoration but our reverent fear. We do not fear him as the pagan should, but we revere him as those who recognize we deserved what the pagan will receive and were spared because of no merit of our own. We do not cower as those who gathered at the foot of Mount Sinai, but we offer profound awe and respect as those who gather at the foot of Mount Zion.

It matters that we revere him, for those who forget the transcendence of God will soon forget his commands. The Old Testament bears repeated witness to this effect. But those who hold in tension the truths of loving Father and just judge will "worship the LORD in the splendor of holiness" (Ps. 96:9). They will bring the acceptable sacrifices of a broken and contrite heart, of obedience, of prayer and worship. It is no accident that Peter alludes to the Passover at this point in his letter (1:19). On that night, the Israelites understood God as both Father and judge, witnessing the angel of death spare them from the judgment that fell on the Egyptians. The Israelites were spared not because of the depth of their faith or the degree of their righteousness, but by the precious blood of the spotless lamb on their doorposts. It was the sole barrier between them and judgment. And so it is for us.

Pointing them to their heavenly Father, Peter reminds his hearers that they are ransomed from the futile ways inherited from their earthly forefathers (1:18). For his Jewish listeners, this would mean freedom from the legalism that was the hallmark of Judaism. For his Gentile listeners, this would mean freedom from the license that characterizes the lives of unbelievers. The old inheritance is set aside. The new inheritance takes its place. The modern listener takes hope in this as well. Each of us comes from a background of legalism or license or, more likely, some combination of the two. But we are not bound to repeat the sin patterns that we inherit from our earthly families. By the grace of our new inheritance in Christ, we can conduct ourselves as the obedient children of our true Father.

In case his hearers should think that Christ was first introduced in the foreshadowing of the Passover lamb of the exodus, Peter assures them that he was foreknown before the foundation of the world itself, and lately revealed (made manifest) to them in the incarnation (1:20). When John the Baptist sees Jesus approach, he declares, "Behold, the Lamb of God, who takes away the sin of the world!" (John 1:29). He connects Christ to the sacrificial system of the old covenant in an unexpectedly expansive way. Whereas one lamb was slain for the sin of each household at Passover, here is one single Lamb who will be slain for the sins of the whole world. In Revelation 13:8 the apostle John speaks of Jesus Christ as "the Lamb slain from the foundation of the world" (KJV).

Peter appeals to this startling truth, this revelation of the Lamb, which was the dearest desire of the prophets to comprehend—this manifestation of grace that defies the understanding of the angels (1 Pet. 1:10–12). He insists that the eternal salvific work of the Son should enable believers to place their faith and hope in God, who raised Jesus from the dead and gave him glory (1:21b). The salvation of the saints was never Plan B. We can trust the One who authors, accomplishes, and applies it for our sake. Our faith lies not in a hastily constructed fall-back scheme, nor do we hope in a God who was blindsided by sin. Our faith and hope rest in the God who made provision for us before uttering the words, "Let there be light" (Gen. 1:3). They rest in the God who is preparing for us a city that "has no need of sun or moon to shine on it, for the glory of God gives it light, and its lamp is the Lamb" (Rev. 21:23). Our faith and hope rest in the God who governs the beginning and the end, and everything between.

Love Earnestly (1:22–25)

Having purified your souls by your obedience to the truth for
a sincere brotherly love, love one another earnestly from a
pure heart, since you have been born again, not of perishable
seed but of imperishable, through the living and abiding word
of God; for

"All flesh is like grass
  and all its glory like the flower of grass.
The grass withers,
  and the flower falls,
but the word of the Lord remains forever."

And this word is the good news that was preached to you.
(1:22–25)

Peter's fourth admonition in light of our inheritance is that we
love one another earnestly. He links obedience to purity of heart,
working itself out practically in the form of brotherly love. The
word "love" is the Greek *agape*, a love that actively chooses its
object, a love of the will. The word "earnestly" connotes depth
and fervency. It describes the way we are loved by God, and it
indicates that we are to love as he has first loved us. God does not
merely tolerate his children but chooses to love them earnestly
with depth and fervency. He commands them to do the same with
one another.

This is not a simple command for the modern listener to follow, and it was not a simple command for Peter's original audience. Persecution from outsiders would have placed strain on the
relationships of insiders. Those who are enduring trials often lash
out at the very people with whom they should share the deepest affection. Peter knows that as their circumstances grow more
difficult, these young believers will be tempted to quarrel among
themselves. But unity in love should be their hallmark.

We see this symptomatic disunity even in the church today,

where infighting among believers increases as the culture around them grows increasingly hostile to their beliefs. When we feel powerless against our adversaries, we are prone to exert power against those closest to us. Peter reminds his hearers that it must not be so among the people of God. Unity in love is the result of actively willing to love one another, not superficially, but earnestly. Brotherly love perseveres when it does not feel like doing so. It chooses to focus on shared essentials rather than squabble over unshared nonessentials. It edifies and encourages, assuming the best about its spiritual siblings, eschewing cynicism and constant critique.

The people of God should earnestly seek unity in love for one another. After all, they have been born again through that which is imperishable, the living and abiding word of God. Peter chooses not one, but two descriptors for this word, and both are worth celebrating. It is a *living* word, alive with the very breath of God; so it has brought us into new life, causing us to be born again. It is an *abiding* word, not passing away like the grass and flowers, but remaining forever. So this word sustains us through this life, training us in holiness and tethering us in hope. Peter declares that this word is the good news that was preached to them, the same good news of Christ into which angels long to look (1:12, 25). This gospel word has saved us, and it continues to save us. Faith in Christ delivered us from the penalty of sin, and it is delivering us from the power of sin as it conforms us to the image of Christ. It gives life and it sustains life.

And it is eternal. To drive home his point about the value of God's living and abiding word in the life of the believer, Peter quotes a passage from Isaiah 40:

> All flesh is like grass
> > and all its glory like the flower of grass.
> The grass withers,
> > and the flower falls,
> but the word of the Lord remains forever. (1 Pet. 1:24–25)

Like a preacher humming the first stanza of "It Is Well with My Soul" during a sermon on enduring trials, Peter gives them only a phrase, but he means to summon to mind the entirety of this prophecy that would have been familiar to his Jewish listeners. Those familiar with the book of Isaiah know that the first thirty-nine chapters are full of God's displeasure over Israel's idolatry, resulting in their exile. But in chapter 40, the tone shifts. The opening lines fall like a rain shower in the desert:

> Comfort, comfort my people, says your God.
> Speak tenderly to Jerusalem,
>   and cry to her
> that her warfare is ended,
>   that her iniquity is pardoned,
> that she has received from the LORD's hand
>   double for all her sins. (Isa. 40:1–2)

It is not until verse 8 of Isaiah 40 that we reach Peter's quoted text, and by then we are immersed in the glorious declaration of the eternal faithfulness of God, which overshadows the transience and inconstancy of humankind, the God who condescends to gather his exiled children and lead them tenderly as a shepherd (Isa. 40:11). Peter, who is writing to a people in exile to give them comfort and encouragement, invokes an ancient message written for a people in exile to give them comfort and encouragement. By choosing to quote this particular passage, Peter says, in essence, *this is not the first time that the people of God have gone into exile, and it will not be the last time the God of all comfort shows up strong and mighty to save.* He chooses an Old Testament prophecy of Christ, the Good Shepherd, tenderly leading his flock.

It would have been a timely word for his original hearers. It is no less a timely word for us today. In the midst of a culture that grows increasingly hostile to our beliefs, we can forget the comfort of a future inheritance. We are habitually prone to concern ourselves with the perishable. We devote our energies to what we will eat or what we will wear, laboring to fill storehouses with that which rusts and is eaten by moths. We take great pains to preserve the youthful appearance of a body that is faithfully declaring to us that we are a mist and a vapor, with every wrinkle we develop and every gray hair we sprout. No, we say, I am not perishing. I am eternal. Behold the work of my hands. We have no time for things of eternal significance, so absorbed are we in the pleasures and cares of this world, which is most certainly passing away.

And what are these things of eternal significance for which we have no time? They are the daily opportunities to "love one another earnestly from a pure heart." Deeply, and fervently, as God has loved us. Naked we came from our mother's womb, and naked we shall return to dust. And the gold and silver that will remain when the last fiery trial of death has been passed will be the earnest love we have invested toward God and others. These are the treasures we store up in heaven. The more focused we are on the perishable, the more diminished will be our ability to invest in the imperishable. But the seed of the imperishable, living, and abiding word of God calls us to live lives of eternal consequence, lives characterized by earnest love for each other, even when we must walk through trial, deprivation, and rejection.

Will we exiles have comfort in this life? No, perhaps not. But comfort comes to those who hope in that which is imperishable, unfading, undefiled, and kept for them in heaven. This is the good news that was preached to us.

Crave the Word (2:1–3)

So put away all malice and all deceit and hypocrisy and envy and all slander. Like newborn infants, long for the pure spiritual milk, that by it you may grow up into salvation—if indeed you have tasted that the Lord is good. (2:1–3)

Having given four admonitions regarding hope, holiness, reverence, and love, Peter now offers a concluding summary thought in the form of a prohibition and an admonition. He tells them to stop practicing (put away) what is sinful and start practicing (crave) what is godly.

The words "put away" translate literally to "put aside," as we would put aside a soiled garment. As a parent, I immediately think of the times that a small child rendered my outfit unwearable due to sickness or an out-of-control diaper. These incidents did not always occur at times or in places where changing my clothes was possible. I know the relief of putting aside a soiled garment. Having earlier admonished us to robe our minds for battle, Peter here describes a disrobing of malice, deceit, hypocrisy, envy, and slander that befits those who call themselves Christians.

Peter wants us to understand that we are not merely to stop doing these things, but to cast them off as disgusting and unclean, with an expectation that we will be relieved to get rid of them. We can infer from the list of negative behaviors that those born again of the living and abiding word would conversely eagerly clothe themselves in a garment not of malice but of goodwill, not of deceit but of truth, not of hypocrisy but of genuineness, not of envy but of generosity, not of slander but of praise. This is the robe worn by the chosen exiles of God, a garment that marks them as aliens and strangers.

Having called his hearers "born again" twice already in the first chapter, Peter now connects their newborn status to their greatest need: pure spiritual milk (2:2). But what is this milk that renders them mature in their salvation? Some translations render the term "pure spiritual milk" as "milk of the word."[2] This makes sense, as Peter has just been talking about the word of the Lord. Like newborns, believers need to feed, and their milk is the living and abiding word of God. They should long for it, or as the NIV says, they should crave it.

---

[2] Both the KJV and the NASB translate the ESV's "pure spiritual milk" (2:2) with "milk of the word." They do this because, as the ESV Study Bible note explains, "'Spiritual' comes from Greek *logikos*, which echoes 'word' (*logos*) of 1:23." *ESV Study Bible*, ed. Wayne Grudem (Wheaton, IL: Crossway, 2008), 2420.

This is a powerful image, familiar to any woman who has nursed a child. Hungry newborns are inconsolable, even frantic, until they latch on to nurse. Newborns are designed to need a mother's milk to survive and thrive. So also, believers are designed to need the pure milk of God's Word, the Bible, to survive and thrive. But any woman who has ever nursed a child will also attest to this: though nothing could be more natural or needful than nursing, getting the hang of it is extremely difficult. It requires perseverance on the part of both the mother and the baby. Though babies need pure milk to survive, they must learn how to receive it.

I find this to be an apt metaphor for Bible study. We know we need to be in the Word to survive and to thrive, and it seems like something so necessary and natural should be effortless to acquire. But it isn't. It requires perseverance on the part of both God and his child. God's perseverance is unquestioned, but our own can flag. We do not expect our time in the Word to require practice, but it does. We must learn how to receive it, through repeated efforts to do so, humbly accepting help.

If we follow Peter's metaphor comparing the imagery of birth and nursing to spiritual rebirth and nourishment, we understand our roles as those commissioned to go and make disciples through a similar lens. It renders every evangelist a metaphorical midwife, helping to deliver newborn believers. It renders every teacher of the Bible a metaphorical lactation consultant, training all believers to feed on that which will grow them to maturity—the pure milk of the Word.

Though modern teachers and preachers may shy away from such intimately maternal metaphors, the Bible does not. Jesus himself seems to have felt no discomfort around issues of female biology, dealing compassionately, for example, with the woman with an issue of blood. And then there is that odd, rarely preached passage in Luke 11:27–28 where Jesus is addressed by a woman in the crowds. Enlivened by his teaching, she cries out, "Blessed is the womb that bore you, and the breasts at which you nursed!"

It's hard for modern ears to imagine someone calling out such a thing in the middle of a sermon. Talk about an awkward moment. In many of our contexts, childbirth happens privately in a hospital, and nursing happens discreetly in a back room. We do not lob these topics into polite conversation. But it was not so in Jesus's day. From their childhood, his followers would have had everyday, firsthand exposure to these "female concerns." Just as when he addressed the woman with the issue of blood, Jesus's response to the woman who cries out indicates no discomfort or rebuke on his part. He capitalizes on her choice of images to draw out a spiritual truth, responding, "Blessed rather are those who hear the word of God and keep it!"

Follow the parallel with me.

She says: "Blessed is the womb that bore you [physical birth], and the breasts at which you nursed! [physical milk]."

He responds: "Blessed *rather* are those who hear the word [spiritual rebirth] and keep it [spiritual milk]."

He responds, in essence, "Do you think it is a blessing to be my mother? Rather, it is a blessing to be reborn into the family of God and nourished to maturity by the words given to us from God." I have to wonder if Peter is not recalling this very scene as he writes to the churches in Asia Minor, "Like newborn infants, long for the pure spiritual milk, that by it you may grow up into salvation."

Blessed are those who have tasted and seen that the Lord is good. Peter concludes his thoughts by invoking a well-known phrase in Psalm 34:8: "Oh, taste and see that the LORD is good!" Apparently, Peter believes that those who have tasted the goodness of the Lord will not be able to get enough of that goodness. Nor, like David in Psalm 34, are they likely to be quiet about the good thing they have found.

Those who experience the goodness of God as revealed in the pure milk of the Word become both its most eager consumers and its most vocal evangelists. They crave that goodness, and they hold it out to others, urging them eagerly to "taste and see!" We will not ask someone else to crave what we ourselves have only a partial appetite for. We will not ask someone else to hope fully in a grace we only partially embrace. But those experiencing difficulty, like Peter's audience, tend to develop a strong appetite for the goodness of the Lord. Why? Because if the Lord is good, then their current circumstance truly is light and momentary. Because if the Lord is good, his judgments can hold no terror for them. If the Lord is good, no trial can hold them forever. If the Lord is good, his sovereignty is cause for rejoicing. If the Lord is good, whatever sorrow or loss they now face will serve his purposes and ultimately result in their joy.

Those who have tasted the goodness of the Lord employ their speech and actions to invite others to the feast. Like the psalmist, they eagerly urge others to "taste and see."

The Incongruous Exile

Hope fully. Be holy. Fear rightly. Love earnestly. What Peter prescribes in 1:13–2:3 is a way of living that is completely incongruous with the wisdom of the world.

Imagine how alien and strange our lives would look if we lived as those who hope fully in Christ. What if our hope were no longer placed on a parent, spouse, child, career, or bank statement? We would be free to give of our time, money, and abilities with no fear of loss. No manipulation or codependency in our relationships. No hoarding of assets or hedging of bets. Completely unlike the people among whom we live.

Imagine how alien and strange our lives would look if we lived as those who strive to be holy as God is holy. What if we truly sought purity of thought, word, and deed? We would meditate on what is true and admirable instead of what is frivolous or perverse. We would speak what is edifying instead of what is destructive. We would do what is good and just instead of what is selfish and self-preserving. No casual dabbling in sin. No negotiating of where the line between holy and unholy lies. Completely unlike the people among whom we live.

Imagine how alien and strange our lives would look if we lived as those who fear God rightly. What if we traded fear of man or fear of failure or fear of loss for right reverence of God? We would strive for the approval of God instead of for the adulation of our peers. We would risk loss of comfort now for the sake of commendation later. No politicking, posturing, or paralyzing insecurities. No self-absorption. Completely unlike the people among whom we live.

Imagine how alien and strange our lives would look if we lived as those who love one another earnestly. What if instead of quarreling and coveting, we lay down our lives for one another after the example of Christ? We would seek the good of others above our own. We would be open-handed and vulnerable, honest about our weaknesses, and humble about our strengths. We would overlook offenses and assume the best about the motives of others. No victim mentality. No self-preservation. Completely unlike the people among whom we live.

We would be, in short, transformed like our unlikely messenger Peter himself, who began by denying his identity as a follower of Christ and ended by identifying with Christ to the point of death. We would be the spiritual exiles Peter envisions, those who know this world is not their home, looking toward the day of Christ's return with eager expectation. We would be those who hold forth the pure milk of the Word, bidding whosoever will to "taste and see!"

Reflect and Pray

Reflect on each question and then take a moment to speak or write the prayers that grow from those reflections.

1. Look back through the various *commands* scattered throughout 1:13–2:3. What parts of this passage make clear the basis on which these commands are given? In other words, in what way is Peter commanding a response to grace rather than an earning of grace?

2. In what ways does this passage encourage you to make application not just individually but *among the body of Christ*? What concrete applications come to mind?

3. This chapter emphasized the importance of "the living and abiding word of God." What are several truths about God's Word that emerge in these verses? In what specific ways do these truths encourage and challenge you?

Think Like an Expositor: Comments from Jen Wilkin

1. On the process of preparing to teach 1 Peter 1:13–2:3:

I enjoyed exploring the imagery that occurred in my particular section. The garment analogies and the newborn-infant imagery presented an added dimension to the teaching that was interesting to explore. I found myself asking, "Do I crave the Word as the text describes or merely show up to teach it?" I meditated on the importance of teaching from my own conviction over sin rather than just dispensing of some academic duty to the text. It's hard to describe that as an enjoyable process, but it was definitely a beneficial one. I also felt challenged and sharpened working collaboratively with the other presenters to make sure the sessions flowed. Typically, I teach through an entire book on my own. Partnering to make sure that the integrity of the message stayed consistent was an enjoyable challenge.

2. On studying context in order to teach the text:

Peter's personal story as recorded in the Gospels and Acts formed a key piece of the context for the passage. Peter is perhaps the most relatable New Testament author, because we know a great deal about his experiences as one of the Twelve. Along with his other colorful interactions with Jesus, his story of restoration after denying Jesus makes him an empathetic teacher. We hear his admonitions to obey, love, forgive, and be humble in a different light because of his firsthand perspective.

Getting a sense of Peter's original audience also shapes our interpretation. Understanding that they were facing uncertainty and danger changes the way we hear Peter's admonitions to them. We know that Peter was willing to follow Christ at great personal cost, so his call to others to do the same can be seen as having been given with full knowledge of its implications. The position of the passage in Peter's letter gives another important layer of context. From a textual standpoint, it matters that Peter does not start with imperatives but with indicatives. We must hear his admonitions in light of the glorious hope he describes in the first twelve verses of his letter. This frames obedience as the reasonable and beautiful response to what God has done rather than as some dry set of commands to be followed.

3. On one aspect of this text that especially moved and challenged you:

Peter's call to love one another earnestly from a pure heart hit me pretty hard. For many years, I read that admonition out of context as a general call to love everyone. Viewing it more pointedly as a call to love my spiritual brothers and sisters caused me to reflect on the current tone of many of our online critiques of one another. If we are going to be gracious with anyone, starting by assuming the best, it should be those within the family of God. I found myself reflecting on how to be faithful in critique (when it is necessary) without becoming a critic. I was challenged by Peter's encouragement to remember the power of an encouraging word. How different would our internal disagreements look and sound if we offered two encouragements for every critique? Peter was a person who knew how to rebuke (and how to be rebuked), yet his letter instructs in a tone that is unmistakably compassionate and encourages in a tone that is unmistakably genuine. I want to be like that.

3

Remember Who You Are!

1 Peter 2:4–10

Carrie Sandom

You may have noticed that in the last couple of years Queen Elizabeth II reached some major milestones. In September 2015 she became the longest-reigning British monarch, and in April 2016 she celebrated her ninetieth birthday. Now, I realize that not everyone is a fan of the British monarchy, but I think most people in the UK, whatever their particular view of the royal family, enjoyed celebrating the queen's birthday. There were a number of photos released to commemorate the occasion. Taken by the American photographer Annie Leibovitz, one of them showed the queen surrounded by her youngest grandchildren and great-grandchildren. William and Kate's daughter, Charlotte, being the youngest, was sitting on the queen's lap, and, standing beside her, one of the other little girls was proudly holding up the queen's handbag. It was a very cute photo—even if the surroundings weren't entirely normal! Not many of us get to take our family photos in the drawing room at Windsor Castle.

One of the boys in the photo was Prince George, looking to all intents and purposes like any other chubby-cheeked two-year-old. (I hope I'm not committing treason by describing him like that!) But, of course, as the years go by, Prince George will come to understand that his particular identity and purpose in life are going to be very different from those of his sister and his cousins. He has a unique connection to the queen that means his destiny will be unlike that of all the other children in that photo. As third in line to the throne, Prince George will one day become king of England and rule over the United Kingdom, Canada, Australia, New Zealand, and all the other realms and territories of the British monarchy—unless, of course, the UK has become a republic by then (which I'm pretty sure is a treasonable thing to say!), but I really don't think that's ever going to happen.

Here in this passage from 1 Peter we're going to see that our identity and purpose in the world are tied to our unique relationship with the Lord Jesus Christ, the King of all kings, queens, and princes. We've seen that Peter wrote this letter to groups of Christians who were scattered over what we know today as Turkey. They were pretty isolated, often on the edge of society, and ostracized by both the Jews who opposed them and the Romans who misunderstood them. Their faith was being tested by all kinds of trials, and they were beginning to learn that they didn't really belong to this world. As Christians today, living in the twenty-first century, we can often feel the same: marginalized and on the edge of our communities, ostracized by the in crowd at college or at work, and often misunderstood by our non-Christian family and friends. Peter wrote this letter to encourage these first-century Christians to stand firm in the true grace of God; we need the same encouragement in our own generation.

God's mercy to us means that we too have been born again into a living hope through the resurrection of Christ. We too have a future inheritance that can never perish, spoil, or fade. And just as Jesus suffered in this world, so too will his people—in every age.

Yes, there is suffering now, but there is also glory to come. And so Peter encourages us to be joyful in our afflictions and faithful in our obedience as we wait for the Lord's return, all the while craving the pure spiritual milk of the living and abiding Word of God.

But do we accomplish these things on our own? There is certainly the need for personal obedience, and it is clear we must individually fight sin in our lives. In this passage, however, Peter introduces the important aspect of our life together as God's people. Indeed, as many of us have discovered, we're not meant to do these things independently.

In 1 Peter 2:4–10, Peter uses two building metaphors to teach us about the Lord Jesus and then spells out the implications of both for all those who belong to him. These building metaphors are universally understood and have wide appeal. *Grand Designs* is a popular TV program in the UK, a bit like *Tiny House Nation* in the United States; the point is that people get to design and then build their dream house. I've never had the opportunity to build my own house, but I guess all of us dream about it—buying a plot of land, sourcing all the materials, laying the foundations, and then watching as the walls and roof follow the architect's plans and complete the shape and design of the building. The apostle Peter gives us pictures of a house that will last forever.

Jesus Is the Living Stone (2:4–5)

> As you come to him, a living stone rejected by men but in the sight of God chosen and precious, you yourselves like living stones are being built up as a spiritual house, *to be a holy priesthood, to offer spiritual sacrifices acceptable to God through Jesus Christ.* (2:4–5)

First, Jesus is a living stone, rejected by men but chosen and precious in the sight of God. Peter reminds his readers that Jesus knows what it is like to be marginalized and rejected by the world; in God's sight, however, he is chosen and precious.

Jesus is a *living* stone—a mixed metaphor to make us stop and think! Stones are normally pretty solid and often very heavy; they are not known for their life and organic properties. But Jesus is a living stone, stable and steadfast, but nevertheless alive. We might think back to the "living hope" of 1 Peter 1:3, a hope based on Jesus's resurrection from the dead.

These verses are full of Old Testament temple imagery. The temple in Jerusalem was hugely significant for the people of Israel under the old covenant. It was an enormously impressive building, constructed with magnificent stones and built on a hill so that everyone could see it. This was where God dwelt with his people, but, because of his holiness, it was also where priests had to offer sacrifices to secure that relationship with him. The temple identified them as God's people and established their corporate life and purpose in the world. But here in this passage Peter reminds these marginalized Christians that their collective identity and purpose in the world are centered on the Lord Jesus Christ. He is the living stone of God's house.

Two implications of this truth are drawn out in verse 5. First, we too are like living stones being built into a spiritual house. The corporate dimension is deliberate. We are all like living stones; we too were once dead but have now been made alive and are being built together into a spiritual house where God dwells by his Spirit. You can't build a house out of just one stone. Many stones are needed. But the stones need to be brought together in one grand design.

When you're building a house you need to buy lots of wood or bricks or stones, and when the building project is finished, there may be some left over, perhaps in a pile nearby. But the leftover bricks and stones are not part of the house. Only the ones that are incorporated into the structure make up the house. We believers are the living stones, made alive in the Lord Jesus and through him built up as a spiritual house. No longer do we need a temple of stones; we are the living temple, united in Christ.

This is an important corrective to our very "me-centered," in-dividualistic culture. The world doesn't revolve around you or me! It revolves around the Lord Jesus Christ. He's the architect of this house, and we are his building materials. We are individually called, but acceptance of that call means we now belong to one another and have an important group identity, the sum of which is more significant than each individual part.

Some people think that if they go to church, then they automatically belong to the Lord Jesus. That's not true, of course. In fact, it's the other way round. You cannot belong to the church unless you first belong to the Lord Jesus. But if you belong to Christ, then you also belong to his church—not just the local church but also the universal church, made up of all God's people from all over the world and through all the centuries. Jesus, the living stone, is building his living stones into a house where God dwells by his Spirit.

This means that we need each other. We cannot live the Christian life on our own. We need to be part of a local church, not just showing up every now and again but fully involved and committed to God's people in that place. We often talk about "going" to church, don't we? But actually, we don't "go" to church like we go to the shopping mall or to the dentist. We don't go to church; we *are* the church. Once we've understood that, it will change the way we think about our brothers and sisters, who are the church with us.

I recently went back to visit the church family where I was working ten years ago. It's a church in central London and full of young people, most of them under the age of thirty-five. To give you some idea of how young everybody is, when I first worked there, the "older" women's group was for women over the age of twenty-seven. On this return visit it was lovely to see my previous church family; of course, they are still my church family, as they are still my brothers and sisters. The Lord has moved me on to serve in another local church since then, but it was great to see how these friends are still walking with the Lord and persevering in all kinds of difficulties and trials.

One of them, a woman called Jill, had been very much on the fringe of things when I was there. But as I talked with her that morning, it was clear to me that something was different; she was now more involved and more committed to the church family. I asked her what had brought about this change, and she told me that her mother had died very suddenly a few years ago, and her father soon after that—and the church family had been wonderful. They'd gathered around and supported and prayed for her in ways she could never have imagined.

It was these family tragedies that had helped Jill to see that she also belonged to another family, a family that was becoming more and more important to her. But then she realized that the time would come when one of the church family would need her support and love and prayers. She said it was as though a light bulb had been turned on in her head: "These people have shown me that I'm part of their family, which means they are part of mine."

What a wonderful testimony to those brothers and sisters in that central London church! They are not just Jill's brothers and sisters; they are ours as well. If we belong to the Lord Jesus, then we belong to each other. Jesus is the living stone, and we too are like living stones being built together into a spiritual house. We have a group identity and purpose that are bound up in him.

There's a second implication of the truth that Jesus is the living stone: we are a holy priesthood offering spiritual sacrifices (v. 5). Again the group dimension is deliberate. We are a holy priesthood (that's our collective identity), and our purpose in the world is to offer spiritual sacrifices to God through the Lord Jesus. Again the metaphor is mixed: not only are we the temple, but we're also the priests offering sacrifices.

Under the old covenant, the priesthood was limited to men from just one tribe, the tribe of Levi. Their role was to serve the Lord, day after day, by offering sacrifices in the temple. This was a reminder to the whole community that sin was a real problem and made relationship with a holy God impossible.

But now, under the new covenant, we know that Jesus is the one true sacrifice for sin; he has established and secured our relationship with God. Now all of God's people (men and women, young and old) from every tribe and nation are a holy priesthood in God's sight. Made holy by the blood of Christ, we are called to serve the Lord not by offering animal sacrifices but by offering spiritual sacrifices, acceptable to God through the Lord Jesus Christ.

What does this all mean for us? It means that how we live in this world matters. We are a holy priesthood, chosen and set apart. We may feel isolated, ostracized, and at times very weak, but we have an important role to play in God's world. Our whole lives are offered up to him. Peter tells us exactly what these spiritual sacrifices are a little later on in the letter, but here's a flavor of what's to come: as God's holy people, we are to resist evil and do good, keeping our conduct honorable; we are called to live as people who are free but not using our freedom as a cover-up for evil; we should endure the pain of unjust suffering without retaliating (just as Jesus did).

Jesus was rejected by the world but is chosen and precious to God. Jesus is the living stone. And, because of him, we too are like living stones, being built into a spiritual house. We are a holy priesthood, offering spiritual sacrifices to God. It's a bit like we're all on the same team with a shared purpose, all working together toward the same goal.

There was a nerve-racking soccer game between England and Wales in the Euro 2016 soccer tournament, the European equivalent to the Copa América. This was the first time Wales had competed in a major tournament in my lifetime—over half a century. Why was it so nerve-racking? Because, being half-English and half-Welsh, I was in two minds about whom to support. Ninety-nine percent of the time, I support England, but I really wanted Wales to win that game. But imagine what would have happened if any of the players on the pitch were in two minds about whom to play for. It would have been a complete disaster. Teams function best when they have a shared identity and a common purpose, with everyone clear about the objectives and working toward the same goal (which, in the case of a soccer match, is really rather important).

And so it is in the church. We need each other. We cannot function as God's people on our own. We have a shared identity and a common purpose in the world, and they are inextricably linked to the Lord Jesus Christ. He is the living stone who gives life to all the rest.

That's the first building metaphor Peter uses in this passage to teach us about the Lord Jesus. The second follows directly from the first.

Jesus Is the Cornerstone (2:6–8)

For it stands in Scripture:

> "Behold, I am laying in Zion a stone,
>   a cornerstone chosen and precious,
> and whoever believes in him will not be put to shame."

So the honor is for you who believe, but for those who do not believe,

> "The stone that the builders rejected
>   has become the cornerstone,"

and

> "A stone of stumbling,
> and a rock of offense."

They stumble because they disobey the word, as they were destined to do. (2:6–8)

In ancient building practices, the cornerstone was the principal stone placed at the base and corner of any building. It was the largest, heaviest, and most carefully positioned stone in the entire structure. It simultaneously established the foundation and determined the course and design of the whole building. Without it, the building was completely unstable and liable to collapse.

Jesus is the *cornerstone* of God's house. He establishes the foundation and design of the whole building. Without him, people have no foundation and no direction in life. He provides both the stability and rationale for God's building, and without him the building will fall.

This metaphor of the cornerstone is used in various Old Testament passages. Peter quotes three of them to remind his readers of its significance. There are wonderful promises here, as well as dire warnings.

The first (in v. 6) comes from Isaiah 28:16, where the Lord God declares:

> Behold, I am the one who has laid as a foundation in Zion,
>> a stone, a tested stone,
> a precious cornerstone, of a sure foundation:
>> "Whoever believes will not be in haste."

Juan Sanchez explains in the introduction that Peter clarifies that last line, explaining that whoever believes in him will not be "put to shame" (1 Pet. 2:6). What a wonderfully reassuring promise that is! However isolated and marginalized these Christians felt, they were established on a firm foundation. Believing in Jesus, the chosen and precious cornerstone, meant they would never be abandoned or forsaken by God. The language of shame here anticipates the day of judgment when all people will have to give an account to God of how they have lived in his world. Those who believe in the Lord will not be shamed on that day; the foundation is secure and will not give way. If Jesus is our cornerstone, we will never stumble and fall.

The second quotation (in v. 7) comes from Psalm 118:22:

> The stone that the builders rejected
>> has become the cornerstone.

What we learn here is that the cornerstone divides people into two groups. Some people accept him, and some reject him. That latter decision will bring an eternity of suffering. During his earthly ministry Jesus applied this verse from Psalm 118 to the chief priests and the Pharisees (Matt. 21:42; Mark 12:10; Luke 20:17); here Peter applies it to all those who reject the Lord Jesus. The stone the builders rejected has become the most important stone of all. Without him there is no foundation and no security on the day of judgment.

The third quotation (in v. 8) comes from Isaiah 8:14, where the Lord declares that he will become "a sanctuary and a stone of offense and a rock of stumbling to both houses of Israel." The stone the builders rejected ultimately brings about their downfall. The reason for this is spelled out at the end of 1 Peter 2:8: they stumble because they disobey the gospel, "as they were destined to do," according to the sovereign foreknowledge of our electing God (cf. 1:1–2). God's Word calls us to repent of our sin and put our faith in the Lord Jesus, but not everyone obeys this call. This was as true in the first century as it is today in the twenty-first. The stakes could not be more clear: those who disobey the gospel are destined to perish.

The Bible clearly teaches that while some people are chosen by God and some are destined to perish, we are all *individually responsible* for how we respond to the gospel. It may seem impossible to grasp how we can hold both these truths together, but that doesn't mean that they are not true. Those who believe in Jesus, who put their trust in him, have a secure foundation and will never be put to shame. They will be honored on the last day (the opposite of being shamed). Those who reject him—who disobey the gospel—will stumble and fall.

A few years ago I was in Atlanta with some friends. We had a few hours to kill and decided to go to the Coca-Cola museum. It was great fun, and we learned a lot about the history of Coca-Cola. Maybe every American knows this already, but Coke was originally sold in pharmacies as a medicinal tonic. It was manufactured in concentrated form, like a thick syrup, and then diluted with soda water and consumed on the premises. Only a few people knew the secret formula of the concentrated syrup—and that, apparently, is still true today.

Part of the attraction of this medicinal tonic was the social interaction of its consumers. Drinking Coke with a group of friends at the local pharmacy became a popular pastime. When the owner was approached about manufacturing the syrup in a diluted form and selling it in bottles so people could enjoy it at home, however, he thought the idea would never catch on. He was so sure of this that he sold the bottling rights for just one dollar. That was in 1899. Twenty years later the company was sold for twenty-five million dollars, and today it is one of the world's most recognizable brands, estimated to be worth about 250 billion dollars. To add insult to injury, when the owner sold the bottling rights, he never actually collected his dollar because he was so sure that the project would fail.

Well, I don't know if you have ever thrown away something that proved to be rather more valuable than you thought, but the bottling rights of Coca-Cola must be right up there as one of the most valuable assets ever to be given away. But such a loss will pale into insignificance compared to what's lost when people reject the Lord Jesus.

Why do people reject him? Think of some of the people you know who have rejected Jesus. What are their reasons? Some I know reject him because they're not convinced he's the Son of God; some think he's irrelevant. Others have rejected him because they don't want to relinquish control of their lives; others don't think they need the forgiveness he offers. One person I know reckons that if there is a judgment to come, he will somehow be able to negotiate his way through it. How foolish is that!

The stone the builders rejected has become the cornerstone—the stone that causes them to stumble and the rock that makes them fall. This means that for anyone reading this who has not yet believed in him, I must implore you to turn to Christ. Turn to him, the living stone. Turn to him for life, a living hope, and a future inheritance.

Turn to him, the cornerstone, who establishes the foundation and design of God's house. Your identity and purpose in the world are inextricably bound up with him and with his people. So put your trust in him and come, join us. "Whoever believes in him will never be put to shame."

But what about those who have already done this, who know that Jesus is the cornerstone and have put their trust in him? Peter spells out two implications for those of us who have become living stones.

But You . . . (2:9–10)

> But you are a chosen race, a royal priesthood, a holy nation, a people for his own possession, that you may proclaim the excellencies of him who called you out of darkness into his marvelous light. Once you were not a people, but now you are God's people; once you had not received mercy, but now you have received mercy. (2:9–10)

First, those who believe in Jesus are *God's treasured possession*. Once again Peter takes imagery from the Old Testament and applies it to the church. The background is Exodus 19, when, after rescuing Israel from Egypt, God met with the people at Sinai and gave them the Ten Commandments. He promised that if they obeyed him fully, they would be his treasured possession, a kingdom of priests, and a holy nation. But they couldn't do it. The law was given to show them how they were to live in the world as God's rescued people—but they couldn't keep it. So ultimately this promise points forward to the Lord Jesus, the true Israel, who perfectly obeys the law and keeps God's commandments.

Here in 1 Peter, the privileges of Jesus's obedience are now applied to the church. If we obey the gospel and believe in the Lord Jesus, then his perfect obedience means that in him we are a chosen race, a royal priesthood, a holy nation, and a people for his own possession. The language of intimacy and belonging is deliberate, and so is the group identity: *together* we are the people of God. *Together* we are chosen, royal, and holy—not because of anything we have done but purely on account of the Lord Jesus, the cornerstone, who establishes both the foundation and the design of God's chosen people. He was chosen and precious to God, and so are we. He was a faithful king and a great high priest, and we too are royal and holy. His perfect obedience becomes the template, the blueprint, and the design for all God's people.

This means, once again, that our identity is inextricably bound up with him. I wonder how you would describe or identify yourself? A twenty-something American woman from the South or maybe a sixty-year-old grandmother from the Midwest? Some might describe me as a British woman who's just teetering on the edge of middle age, but actually none of these things really describe me or even matter that much. When we become Christians, our nationality, our gender, and our age are not what define us. If we believe in the Lord Jesus, then we are first and foremost God's people, chosen and precious to him; we are a treasured possession, not a one-dollar purchase but something much more valuable; we are a royal priesthood and a holy nation. Christians are a people who belong to Christ and find their identity and purpose in him.

One of my former colleagues in the UK speaks of the special privilege he's had of twice being adopted into a new family. He was adopted by his parents at the age of seven and can remember arriving at his new home where he was completely amazed to discover that he now had a bedroom all to himself. And when his mom took him into his new school, he was overjoyed to hear her say to his teacher, "This is my son, Rupert." He had never been called anyone's son before, and it took him a while to really believe that he now belonged to a family that counted him as one of their own.

But then some years later Rupert became a Christian and discovered that he had been adopted all over again—this time into God's family. And membership in this family would last forever, into all eternity. The security of knowing that his heavenly Father had chosen him and would love him and count him as his own forever was completely overwhelming and yet reassuringly familiar. He'd been adopted for life already, but now he had the extra privilege of being adopted for all eternity.

And so it is with us. Christian believers are God's treasured possession and have been adopted into God's family. We are a chosen race, a royal priesthood, a holy nation, not because of anything we have done but because of God's mercy. Peter picks up on themes from the prophet Hosea when he says: "Once you were not a people, but now you are God's people; once you had not received mercy, but now you have received mercy" (v. 10; see Hos. 2:23). How wonderful to know that on the last day, we will stand before the throne of God and will hear him say, "They're mine, they belong to me!"

But this new collective identity brings with it a new purpose. Here's the second implication of our being living stones: we are *called to proclaim God's glory* (v. 9). He has called us out of darkness into his wonderful light. This is the message of the gospel, and he wants us to proclaim it to the world—with our lips when we meet together and sing his praise but also with our lives of spiritual sacrifice all the week long.

These Christians may have looked weak and fragile in the eyes of the world, but they were specially chosen instruments in the eyes of the Lord. They were his Christ-empowered means of proclaiming God's glory in that corner of the world. And the same is true for us. We are his chosen people, a treasured possession, rescued from the kingdom of darkness and brought into his marvelous light. We are God's chosen means of proclaiming his glory in the world.

When we meet together as God's people, we may not look very impressive, but we have a message to proclaim that can raise people from the dead and give them a living hope and a heavenly inheritance. We have a message that can ransom sinners from futile ways and purify their souls; a message that can stop them stumbling and ensure that they will never be put to shame; a message that can rescue them from darkness and bring them into God's marvelous light. We are God's chosen people, and this is the purpose we have in the world.

Do you hear the urgency of all this? We have a collective identity and purpose that are inextricably bound up with the Lord Jesus Christ. We are living stones being built together into a spiritual house; we are a holy priesthood offering spiritual sacrifices to God; and we are his treasured possession called to proclaim his glory in the world. We need to keep coming to Jesus, and we need to keep believing in him. We need to let him establish the foundation and course of our lives together as God's people, for we belong to each other, and we need each other. We need to live our lives for him, resisting evil and doing good. We need to let him mold the course and direction that our lives take, following the path he took, even if it leads to unjust suffering and reproach from the world. And we need to proclaim God's glory in the world, just as he did.

There are people in our families, our communities, and our workplaces, who have no idea that Jesus is the living stone who can give them living hope and build them into his house. They have no idea that Jesus is the cornerstone who can give them a secure foundation and true identity and purpose in the world. If they reject him, they will stumble and fall on the last day. So we must tell them. This is what we've been given to do as God's chosen and precious people in the world.

Prince George has a unique identity and purpose that is inextricably bound up with his relationship with the queen. And we too have a unique identity and purpose that is inextricably bound up with the Lord Jesus Christ, the King of all kings. May we be those who rejoice in the fact that our identity and purpose in the world are inextricably bound up with our relationship with Christ. May we be those who delight in the knowledge that we are chosen and precious to God and together are being built up as a spiritual house. May we be those who understand that we have been called out of darkness and into his marvelous light, and may we seek to proclaim this gospel to others so that they too might believe and become part of God's house, firmly established on the Lord Jesus Christ—the chosen and precious living stone.

Reflect and Pray

Reflect on each question and then take a moment to speak or write the prayers that grow from those reflections.

1. This chapter focused on the *identity* of God's people. What are some of the ways in which you or people you know struggle with issues of identity? In what ways does 1 Peter 2:4–10 speak right into these struggles?

2. Muse on that picture of a *spiritual house of living stones*, as Peter presents it in 2:4–8. How would you summarize the place of Jesus in this house? What aspects of this picture especially strike you or encourage you?

3. This chapter emphasized the call to *proclaim God's excellencies*. In light of the context in verses 9–10, what exactly does that mean? What makes answering this call a challenge in your life? What are some specific ways you might even more faithfully answer this call?

Think Like an Expositor: Comments from Carrie Sandom

1. On the process of preparing to teach 1 Peter 2:4–10:

The most crucial part of my preparation was seeing how this passage fits into the wider context of 1 Peter. Questions such as "How does this passage connect with what comes before and afterward?" and "What would we lose if this passage wasn't in 1 Peter?" were uppermost in my mind as I worked on the text. Peter has told us why he is writing this letter (1 Pet. 5:13: stand firm in the true grace of God), and the key application verses come just after this section, in 2:11–12. As a result, it was important to see how 1 Peter 2:4–10 encourages us to remember God's grace (he has called us out of darkness into his marvelous light), to stand firm in it (once you were not a people, but now you are God's people), and to live honorably among the Gentiles (offer spiritual sacrifices and proclaim God's excellencies).

That said, one of the greatest challenges was to keep the focus of the talk on Jesus and not make this passage all about us. The passage certainly has application for us but only after we've understood certain truths about the Lord Jesus (see below). Another challenge was how much of the Old Testament background to include: the temple imagery is strong, but the three quotations explaining the cornerstone from Isaiah 28, Psalm 118, and Isaiah 8 are also important.

The most enjoyable part was working on the text and using its building metaphors to shine the spotlight on the Lord Jesus. Without him there is no foundation or structure to God's house; in fact there is no house!

2. On identifying the structure of the passage in order to teach the text effectively:

First, I looked for repeated words and phrases: *living stone* or *stones*; *chosen and precious*; *cornerstone*; *holy*; *believe* or *believes*; *stumble* or *stumbling*; *people*. These help to determine the central themes of the passage.

Then I looked for linking words at the start of phrases or sentences to see how they join the passage together. For example: "As you come to him" (v. 4; this is what we do in light of what we learn about Jesus here); "For it stands in Scripture" (v. 6; the "for" works like a "because" and gives a reason for what has just been taught in vv. 4–5); "So the honor is for you" (v. 7; the "so" acts as a "therefore" and draws out the implications of what has just been said in v. 6 about not being put to shame); "But you are a chosen race" (v. 9; the "but" sets up a contrast with those who stumble in v. 7); "Once you were not . . . but now you are" (v. 10; another contrast, repeated twice for emphasis).

The next stage was to work out the main teaching points of the passage, based on the main points about Jesus that emerge. Keeping Jesus as the focus of each teaching point was a deliberate attempt to show that the passage is really all about him and that our identity and purpose in the world are inextricably bound up with our relationship with him. Each of the two points about Jesus has two implications for us:

1. Jesus is the living stone (v. 4)
   ⇨ We too are like living stones being built into a spiritual house (v. 5)
   ⇨ We are a holy priesthood offering spiritual sacrifices (v. 5)

2. Jesus is the cornerstone (vv. 6–8)
   ⇨ We are God's treasured possession (vv. 9–10)
   ⇨ We are called to proclaim God's glory (v. 9)

The structure discerned in the passage then became the structure of the talk.

3. On one aspect of this text that especially moved and challenged you:

We never study God's Word in a vacuum. We are always in a particular stage of life and health (both physical and spiritual), and our relationship with the Lord is never static. My mother died a few months before I gave this talk, so I was grieving her loss as I prepared. She was a huge part of my life and the hub of our family life, so, while I know she is now safely home with the Lord, her absence has left a big hole. This passage was a real encouragement to me as I grieved, because it reminded me that I belong to another family, to God's family, and we are treasured by him and precious to him.

The main challenge came from the reminder that our life together as God's people is corporate. We are being built into God's house together, and we are called to proclaim God's glory together. We live in a very individualistic culture and are encouraged to see ourselves as the center of everything we do, but there is only one person at the center of the universe, and that's the Lord Jesus. Our life and purpose in the world are defined by our relationship with him; that means we are inextricably linked to each other. I have become more thankful and more prayerful for my church family as a result.

4

Following Jesus Far from Home

1 Peter 2:11–3:12

Mary Willson

The apostle Peter shows us how God calls us out of darkness into his marvelous light and how he calls us to go right back into that dark world, shining his light. But the way Peter instructs us to shine God's light may surprise us. In fact, few New Testament ethical texts jar us more than 1 Peter 2:11–3:12. Peter's words arrest us because they're so counterintuitive to the way our society thinks about who we are and why we're here.

I recently walked through my local bookstore to browse the prominent titles on display in the religion and self-help sections. Many of the titles I saw expressed something of what our society believes about human identity and purpose. According to these authors and publishers, we are autonomous spiritual beings who control our own future. We sit in the driver's seat and can steer our life toward power, success, and independence—the supreme values and aspirations of our age.

Peter's instruction in 1 Peter 2:11–3:12 paints a radically different picture. He shows us two characteristics of the true believer that set her apart from the world: namely, her status and her conduct. He first notes our distinctive status as believers—who we are in this world (2:11a). Then he addresses how therefore we are to conduct ourselves (2:11b–12) and how to live out this new conduct in four different relational contexts (2:13–3:12).

1. Our Status (2:11a)

Let's examine first what Peter says about our status. He begins with that simple but all-important word: "beloved." Some English translations have "dear friends," but the word is simply *beloved*. Beloved by whom? These believers are beloved by Peter, to be sure, but far more importantly they're beloved by God himself (cf. 1 Pet. 2:10). And so are all of us who have put our faith in Christ. We are God's Spirit-born children, members of the family of the triune God.

And we're beloved "sojourners and exiles." We're just traveling through. This world is not our home. In fact, we're far from home. We live here in tents, not castles. In order to live the Christian life we must set our hearts on our true home, not on the things of this world. This is vital, and entirely contrary to the way most people relate to this world. As a human race we're always seeking to settle down, to get comfortable, to find security, and to make our way to success in this world. But Peter says Christians aren't like that; rather, we're like the faithful Jews in their exile in Babylon. They lived responsibly in Babylon, but they desperately wanted to return to Jerusalem, the city of God. So too as we live our life in this world as aliens and strangers, we must long for the New Jerusalem promised us in Revelation 21. And our ultimate citizenship there determines how we conduct ourselves here.

Not too long ago, I spent time overseas with a friend whose

husband is a diplomat in a foreign country. Their status as ambassadors of their country in a foreign land affects almost everything about their lives; it determines not only how he spends his time during business hours but also how they relate to the people in their apartment building, how they strategize about evangelism, and how they interact with waiters at restaurants. Their vocational effectiveness depends upon embracing their strangeness and putting it to use for the good of that particular foreign country in which they serve. As Christians we have to embrace our strangeness too. We can't really begin to live the Christian life in this world until we understand our Christian status in this world.

Sometimes it's when we face hardship that we're tempted to forget who God has made us to be. And we do face hardship. Internal forces "wage war" against our soul (2:11). And external forces assail us: people who misunderstand us and speak against us (2:12). And the Devil himself prowls around like a roaring lion looking to devour us (5:8). We struggle in this place against the world, the flesh, and the Devil.

The "elect exiles" (1:1) in Asia Minor to whom Peter writes felt these tensions. They were misunderstood and despised by their culture on account of their identification with Jesus. In his application Peter focuses on the most socially vulnerable Christians and the grueling circumstances they might face because of their faith. Peter's not interested in an anesthetized portrait of the Christian life. He applies this new status in Christ to the verbally bullied, the socially and politically disenfranchised, the physically and emotionally weary, the lonely, the vulnerable, and the reviled.

He applies this status to you and to me.

Some of us are in situations that feel utterly desperate. Because of our Christian convictions, people whom we love misunderstand us. Because we don't endorse certain cultural values, society calls us hypocritical and hateful people. And because year after year we may have wrestled with the same old sins and the same old brokenness, we feel beaten down. These situations can be truly dark. But the darkest, most complicated circumstance in your life can become the very platform upon which God most brilliantly displays his mighty strength.

We're far from home, yes, but we're not far from him. It's true that you're an alien and a stranger. It's true that you may have to face cancer or betrayal or the loss of a loved one. You might lose your job or fail an exam. But you will never face the withdrawal of God's love for you. Your permanent status is "beloved of God." Your unchangeable identity is "beloved citizen of the city of God."

Are you quite sure you've received this distinct status? Do you belong to him and to his kingdom? And if so, do you see yourself as a sojourner in this world who is dearly loved by the Lord? Perhaps some of us need to ask God to grant us for the first time this new identity in Christ or else to remind us again of the identity he's given us. Please don't miss this opportunity today.

Now, notice in our text that this God-given status is the foundation upon which all subsequent discussion of Christian conduct must rest. It's as beloved sojourners that we heed this instruction. The Scriptures always make explicit the logical priority of Christian identity before Christian ethics.

2. Our Conduct (2:11b–3:12)

At the same time, our distinct identity must lead to a distinct way of life. So the second major observation here is that we are a people with a peculiar conduct that is based upon our peculiar status. We're following Jesus far from home. We're not aimless wanderers. We're people on a mission to glorify God in a strange land.

Let's take a moment to observe Peter's flow of thought. In 2:11–12, Peter establishes the key themes of his whole exhortation. This is the way we might summarize his central idea about how we follow Jesus far from home: as beloved sojourners, resist evil and do good for the glory of God. But Peter doesn't just tell us to resist evil and do good; he shows us how. In 2:13–3:12 he applies these principles to four representative relationships. Beloved sojourners resist evil and do good for the glory of God in civic life (2:13–17), in professional life (2:18–25), in marital life (3:1–7), and in all of life (3:8–12).

Two Principles (2:11b–12)

How do we follow Jesus far from home? We do two things. The first one is negative: we resist evil. The second is positive: we do good. Or to use Peter's language, we abstain from fleshly passions, and we conduct ourselves honorably. These are two sides of the same coin: turning from evil and embracing good. And we do this because of who we are: beloved sojourners.

Let's first examine the negative: we resist evil (2:11). We have nothing to do with the passions of the flesh. What are these "passions of the flesh"? Peter is talking about lusts of the body and mind, those drives and desires that oppose the fruit of the Spirit such as anger, envy, greed, and pride. He describes these passions of the flesh as aiming to destroy our souls. In this place far from home, we cannot forget that we are in the midst of war. And the war is not just out there; it's within us. Even the passions of our own flesh attack us, and we must engage this spiritual battle with the weapons God provides.

Now notice the positive dimension: we do good. We "keep [our] conduct among the Gentiles honorable" (2:12). By "Gentiles" here, Peter most likely means those who don't profess faith in Jesus Christ. We engage in society with all sorts of people who have all sorts of beliefs, and as we do so, we adopt a way of life that is noticeably good to them.

But why do we abstain, and why do we do good? For the glory of God: "so that when they speak against you as evildoers, they may see your good deeds and glorify God on the day of visitation" (2:12).[1]

---

[1] Here we find a clear echo of Jesus's exhortation in the Sermon on the Mount, "Let your light shine before others, so that they may see your good works and give glory to your Father who is in heaven" (Matt. 5:16). Other portions of 1 Peter 2:11–3:12 also indicate Peter's deep reflection upon his personal experience with Jesus and upon the Scriptures (e.g., in 2:22–25 his application of Isaiah's suffering servant passage to Jesus's vicarious suffering).

Our behavior in public and in private should show the truthfulness of the Christian message we proclaim, despite the efforts of those who may slander us. Perhaps the truth won't be made clear in our lifetime but certainly on the day of visitation—the day when God will come to judge the living and the dead. On that day every creature will glorify God, whether through condemnation or through salvation. And how we long to see people glorify God by turning to Christ in faith: people from every tribe, tongue, and nation; people who have grown up in the church; people who have never set foot in a church building; people who are presently hostile to the gospel and even murdering Christians. Because we love God and because we love lost people, we rejoice to live out our Christian identity in full view of this world, appealing to people through our lips and our lives to be reconciled with their Maker. Peter shows us that there is a great deal at stake in the way we conduct ourselves in this life.

Four Contexts (2:13–3:12)

Now, let's get practical, because that's exactly what the apostle Peter does at this point. He addresses four theaters of our lives in which we live out this peculiar conduct.

Civic Life (2:13–17). In civic life, beloved sojourners resist evil and do good for the glory of God. These first-century Christians in Asia Minor knew the complexities and costs of identifying with Christ in the public square. Peter wasn't writing to the culture shapers of the day. His readers, a tiny minority in the Roman Empire, felt oppressed, fearful, and disenfranchised within a corrupt political social system. That resonates with us. Many of us increasingly feel unprotected or undervalued by our political systems. Our culture often sees the public articulation of Christian principles as an infringement upon others' civic freedoms. And so we must now endure frequent ignorant and unfounded accusations against Christianity.

When we're treated unfairly, the passions of our flesh rage, and we're tempted to indulge them in one of three ways. Sometimes we fight, often on social media. We view public figures or systems as our ultimate enemies, perhaps because we've bought the lie that our stories are bound up in the stories of this world—of the rise and fall of nations, institutions, and even certain constitutional liberties we hold dear. We've forgotten that the Christian's story is the story of the kingdom of Christ. Sometimes we flee. We form a holy huddle and quarantine ourselves from our neighbors who we suspect disapprove of our convictions. Our Bible studies become exclusive clubs, with no seats regularly filled by unbelievers. We spend all our time within the confines of our Christian community and thereby have no way of keeping our conduct honorable among the Gentiles. Other times we conform. We don't like being sojourners and exiles, and so we do everything we can to minimize our strangeness. We just want to be liked and accepted by our friends and neighbors. We claim that our Christian "freedom" means we can live just like everybody else. We become more interested in demonstrating reasonableness according to the standards of our age than in demonstrating holiness according to the standards of God.

But when we forfeit our distinct status in this world, we forfeit the very purpose of our existence. As Malcolm Muggeridge was known to say, "Never forget that only dead fish swim with the stream." No, instead of fighting, fleeing, or conforming, we must resist evil and do good in civic life. Peter writes, "Be subject . . . to every human institution" (2:13). He calls us to submit voluntarily to imperfect, and sometimes unjust, civil authorities, giving them no legitimate reason to punish us. And then: "Honor everyone. Love the brotherhood. Fear God. Honor the emperor" (2:17). Notice that we don't fear the emperor; we fear God. We honor the emperor, just like we honor everyone else. And we must honor everyone. Imagine how radical it would be if each of us obeyed that one little command. We may be tempted to think, "Surely this command to honor everyone doesn't apply to politicians whose policies I despise, or to comment sections on blogs, or to family members who complicate our lives." But we can't escape those little words,

"Honor everyone," not least as we recall how costly this command would have been for Peter's original audience and those specific rulers, such as Nero, to whom Peter calls them to submit.

So Peter urges rightful submission to duly established human authorities and respect for all people—both of which express an underlying fear of God. This means there must be respect and prayers from every believer in the United States for our chief civil officers, whether or not their political policies align with our own.

We do this "for the Lord's sake" (2:13), and because it is "the will of God" that we silence false accusations by doing good rather than by retaliating (2:15). God has chosen to reveal his character to oppressors through our good conduct in the midst of oppression. We don't use the freedom Christ has secured for us by his blood as an excuse to lead whatever sort of lives we want or to say whatever we want about people. No, God has set us free to serve (2:16).

This means that instead of merely searching for every possible loophole on our taxes, which we are free to do, we voluntarily give to the poor; instead of simply establishing protected communities and schools for ourselves, which we are free to do, we take our family to help some under-resourced third graders learn how to read; instead of only calling the mayor's office to complain about our delinquent garbage pickup, which we are free to do, we write letters to public officials thanking them for their faithful service. The Word of God says: Don't use your freedom as a cover-up for evil, but live as servants of God.

Now, at this point we have to make an important qualification. Sometimes a federal or local government defies God's standards and demands obedience from its citizens in a way that would violate their conscience. Peter himself encountered this sort of challenge when the authorities tried to keep him from preaching Christ (cf. Acts 4:19–20). Many of us have celebrated the recent decision to put on our United States currency the image of Harriet Tubman, who led hundreds of African American slaves to freedom in the nineteenth century. We're memorializing her because she had the courage to defy a government in the areas it defied God. And we know from her own accounts that she did this because of her ultimate allegiance to God.[2] We too relate to civic authorities as God-fearers. Christians across the ages have engaged in nonviolent civil disobedience, exercised in obedience to our Lord Christ. And in our day, as we press for social justice and for political and legal reform—especially advocating for the poor and marginalized— we must always exhibit a relentless commitment to submit respectfully when our conscience allows. We must honor everyone.

Professional Life (2:18–25). Peter now turns to a second context in which we live out our distinctive conduct. In professional life, beloved sojourners resist evil and do good for the glory of God (2:18–25). Here he addresses the weakest members of society, the household servants. Household servants were slaves, and although first-century slavery was radically different from the race-based slavery practiced in the United States, it was still slavery. These men and women were subject to the whims of their masters. Life would have been grueling for many of them, especially those who had masters hostile to the Christian faith, who may have resented their slaves' newfound religious convictions.

First-century slavery shouldn't be equated with twenty-first-century Western workplaces. But it seems to me that we can glean some general principles from this passage about submission to authorities in the workplace. Whether we're accountants or social workers, most of us work under authority. We have supervisors. And sometimes they create a lot of problems for us. They might mismanage us, undercut us, even openly mock us on account of our faith. When this happens, we usually feel powerless. When we feel degraded in our workplace, we're tempted to retaliate. Maybe we try to get even with our boss by gossiping about her with our colleagues. Or maybe we don't do our best work for that assignment

---

[2] See, for example, Sarah H. Bradford's *Scenes in the Life of Harriet Tubman* (Auburn, NY: W. J. Moses, 1869), 20.

we deem to be unreasonable. Or maybe we do everything we're supposed to do, but grudgingly.

But when we're living out our distinct Christian identity in this world, we refuse to repay evil for evil. Instead, we commit ourselves to do good. Peter urges submission irrespective of a master's character (2:18). Then he gives us four reasons for obeying such a command even when it's costly (2:19–25). He signals each of these reasons with the little word "for" (vv. 19, 20, 21, 25).

These are difficult instructions. Humanly speaking, they're impossible. And yet these instructions about patiently enduring injustice lie at the heart of all our Christian conduct. So how do we do it? We remember who we are: servants of the living God. And we remember whom we aim to please in all things: our Master, the Lord Jesus himself. This is massively practical in our professional life.

The late Howard Hendricks used to tell a story about a time when he was on an airplane, and there was a very long delay on the tarmac.[3] A man sitting near him grew impatient and eventually gave the flight attendant all kinds of trouble, but she consistently responded to him with grace and helpfulness. Hendricks was so amazed by the flight attendant's professionalism that he stayed in his seat while the other passengers deplaned just so he could thank her. He said something like, "Ma'am, please tell me your name so that I can write to your airline and commend you for your wonderful performance today." She kindly responded, "Thank you, sir, but I don't work for the airline." He was obviously startled by this. Then she said, "I work for Jesus Christ." This woman graciously endured hardship in her workplace because she understood what Peter is saying here: we're following none other than the Lord Jesus Christ.

So we live out these instructions by remembering who we are and whom we aim to please, and, above all, by remembering who

---

[3] This story has been passed on informally through Dr. Hendricks's students. My father recalled hearing it and passed it on to me.

he is. Peter writes, "For this is a gracious thing, when, mindful of God, one endures sorrows while suffering unjustly" (2:19). Mindful of God. Christians persevere in the face of opposition by remembering God and actively relying upon him. The very Spirit who raised Jesus Christ from the dead is near us when we call and supplies us with strength and grace. And he is pleased with us when we endure injustice: "for this is a gracious thing in the sight of God" (2:20).

We don't have to imagine what this way of life might look like. We're not operating in the hypothetical. We've been given a perfect example to follow: Jesus himself. The word for "example" in 2:21 draws upon the idea of a child's grammar book that helps her learn to write the letters of the alphabet by tracing over them. Jesus is our pattern. We trace our lives in him.[4] Following in his steps leads us on the path of the consummate beloved sojourner—the one who voluntarily left heaven's splendor to identify with us and make his home in our world of suffering; the one who did not count equality with God a thing to be grasped, but made himself nothing, taking on the very nature of a servant.

As a beloved sojourner, Jesus resisted evil his whole life, even when fiercely tempted in the wilderness directly by Satan. Jesus secured sinlessness by rigorous, daily battle against all that waged war upon him—the full arsenal of his enemies. And he did good, keeping his conduct honorable among the Gentiles. He fed the hungry, welcomed the sinner, comforted the grieving, taught the wayward. And he did all this out of love for his Father and love for broken and lost people.

But this beloved sojourner's commitment to resist evil and do good culminates in his journey to the cross. These footprints lead us to the place of the skull, the place of excruciating suffering on account of his faithfulness. On that journey, Jesus submitted himself utterly to his Father. And—this is astounding—he also submitted himself to crooked, cruel earthly authorities.

---

[4] Karen H. Jobes, *1 Peter*, Baker Expository Commentary on the New Testament (Grand Rapids, MI: Baker, 2005), 195.

Peter can close his eyes and see this all like it was yesterday. He had been there. He followed Jesus at a distance (Matt. 26:58).[5] This sinless Son of God was falsely accused. He was reviled. He was spat upon. He was violated. He was shamed publicly, hanging naked on a cursed tree.[6] Yet he was silent. He refused to retaliate. How? He "continued entrusting himself to him who judges justly" (1 Pet. 2:23). Jesus was mindful of God. He had faith that though he would be found guilty in the courts of men, he would be vindicated in the court of his Father.

He lays out the pattern for you and me: "If anyone would come after me, let him deny himself and take up his cross and follow me. For whoever would save his life will lose it, but whoever loses his life for my sake will find it" (Matt. 16:24–25). This is our calling. In one of Scripture's most explicit passages about a Christian's principal vocation, the paradigm is the cross.[7]

But we can't stop here. Peter shows us the example we must follow, yes, but he anchors this in the gift we must receive: "He himself bore our sins in his body on the tree. . . . By his wounds you have been healed" (2:24). We follow Jesus not simply because he has modeled a way of life for us. We follow him because he has endured all this sorrow, all this suffering, for us and for our salvation. Jesus, the suffering servant, must be our Savior before he can become our example. If we don't receive his substitutionary sacrifice on our behalf, his example crushes us. An example can't remedy our deepest predicament. An example can't liberate us to die to sin and live to righteousness. No, "the whole head is sick,

---

[5] As Peter retells the events of Christ's passion in this passage, he draws from the suffering servant prophecy of Isaiah 53 and from his own eyewitness experience.

[6] In his vivid description of Jesus's sin-bearing "on the tree" in 2:24, Peter most likely alludes to Deut. 21:23, indicating that Jesus has borne the curse of the law in our place (cf. Gal. 3:13). In light of the present context, it is not insignificant that Jesus died a slave's death, as the Romans were known to punish slaves with crucifixion. Consider Jesus's profound identification with the socially weakest members of these churches in Asia Minor. Moreover, Peter commends the believing slaves' patient endurance of injustice as the model of righteous suffering for the whole congregation.

[7] After indicating how Peter would die, Jesus's last recorded words spoken directly to Peter were, "Follow me" (John 21:19). Such cruciformity is not reserved for Peter, however; the apostle Paul writes, "I die every day!" (1 Cor. 15:31). When we resist evil and do good after the pattern of Jesus, we will suffer. Yet this suffering is a privilege, since in it we share in Christ's sufferings (1 Pet. 4:13).

and the whole heart faint" (Isa. 1:5). We must have a "Shepherd and Overseer" who lays down his life to heal us, his straying sheep (1 Pet. 2:25; cf. Isa. 52:13–53:12).

Peter knows that Jesus's death was for him. He had rebuked Jesus for speaking about the necessity of his suffering (Matt. 16:22). He had denied Jesus three times in Jesus's hour of great agony (Matt. 26:69–75). This is why Peter can write with such conviction about the call to bless those who persecute us—because Peter, the Christ rebuker, the Christ denier, knows that he's the persecutor who's received God's everlasting blessing.

And if we would be servants who follow these footsteps, we must know that Jesus's death is for us. We must experience personally the truth about which the hymnist writes: "Ashamed, I hear my mocking voice / Call out among the scoffers. / It was my sin that held Him there / Until it was accomplished."[8] Unless we reckon with the fact that we were those revilers, we were those persecutors, we will never extend true mercy to those who revile us nor forgive those who bring suffering in our life. We do all this in and through Jesus Christ. We don't do this in our own strength. We can submit to imperfect civic and workplace authorities because we trust in God.

Marital Life (3:1–7). Peter now mentions a third crucial context for our distinctly Christian conduct: marital life (3:1–7). And in marital life, beloved sojourners resist evil and do good for the glory of God. Peter once again pastorally addresses some of the most vulnerable members of these congregations (3:1–6). He knows that for Christian women, marital submission to an unbelieving man is severely challenging.

Some of you women readers know the pain and complication of being married to a man who isn't following the Lord Jesus—who, as Peter writes, is disobedient to the word (3:1). Some of you have been praying for years, for decades, that God would remove your

---

8 Stuart Townend, "How Deep the Father's Love for Us" (n.p.: ThankYou Music, 1995).

husband's heart of stone and grant him a heart of flesh. Maybe you're tired. Maybe you feel profoundly alone. May God comfort you today that your story is right here, embedded in God's inspired Word as a situation in which he delights to work. And he embeds us in a body of believers, even the whole company of saints across redemptive history who have hoped in God in the midst of hardship, like Sarah.

So even in this intimate form of suffering, we follow Jesus far from home. Those of you in this situation know that it requires an ongoing, deliberate commitment to resist evil. Peter addresses at least three temptations in this passage. Sometimes in our marriage we're tempted to use words in unhelpful ways. Maybe we think we can force our husbands to change by arguing with them. Or maybe we retaliate against them with our words, disrespecting them overtly or passive-aggressively. Perhaps this temptation is all the more acute for those of us who are married to men who at one time professed faith in Christ but have wandered from the way or who have abdicated their responsibilities as husbands and/or fathers.

Other times we're tempted to distract ourselves from our pain with the external and the material. Whether married or single, many of us feel dissatisfied in our station in life. And it can be so tempting to hush that loud cry of our hearts with stuff. Stuff can give us an illusion of that control we so desperately crave. Have a bad day at work? Go buy some new shoes! Just got rejected by another guy? Get on social media and post that striking picture of yourself from spring break! When we're most aware of our inadequacies, we're most tempted to find significance in our hair, our jewelry, our clothes, our bank accounts, our academic degrees, the "success" of our children, the "success" of our ministry. We adorn ourselves with these things so that our lives will feel full, but we do it because we feel so empty.

Sometimes we're tempted to crumble in fear and anxiety. The women in this situation in Peter's day certainly might have reason to be afraid, humanly speaking. Though some women enjoyed a certain level of independence, generally in that culture a wife was expected to adopt her husband's religion and obey him in all things. For a Christian woman, for example, to refuse to violate her conscience by worshiping her husband's false god might have provoked anger from him. Maybe he would have spoken harshly with her, maybe he would have threatened her, or maybe he would have forced her into isolation or other truly frightening things. In such circumstances, it would have been easy to drown in fear.

The gospel shows us a better way. We resist evil—these temptations to rely on our words, to distract ourselves with the external, or to live in fear. And we do good, committing ourselves to follow in the footprints of Christ. Peter writes, "Be subject to your own husbands" (3:1). This is not a general command for women to be subject to all men. Peter calls for a wife to submit to her own husband, with the result that "they may be won without a word" (3:1). Her ordinary, ongoing, respectful conduct commends to her husband the love of Christ, after the pattern of Christ.

Rather than distracting ourselves with the superficial, Peter urges, "Let your adorning be the hidden person of the heart with the imperishable beauty of a gentle and quiet spirit, which in God's sight is very precious" (3:4). God's sight—others may not see our faithful following in his steps, one foot in front of the other day by day, moment by moment, but God sees us. The beauty of a Christ-following heart is precious to him and will never fade away. Peter points to the examples of such hearts among centuries of "holy women who hoped in God"—like Sarah, who in the midst of all kinds of obstacles and difficulties, still submitted to her husband, addressing him respectfully as "lord." She certainly didn't do it perfectly! And neither will any of her "children" (1 Pet. 3:6). But such a heart of submission, ultimately to Christ our Lord, is a heart free from enslavement to fear. Fear cannot take root in the hearts of women who hope in God (cf. 1 Pet. 1:13) and, as a result of this hope, "do good and do not fear anything that is frightening" (1 Pet. 3:6).

Now some object to Peter's language here in verse 6 because they claim it somehow sanctions wicked behavior on the part of the husband, as if Peter minimizes the evil of a man abusing his wife. However, God does not call a woman to subject herself to anything that violates her Christian conscience, including willingly submitting to a husband's violence against her. I recognize that some of you reading this now have experienced the evil of domestic abuse and the pain, the horror, and the loneliness it so often brings. Peter is not commanding that we let anyone abuse us in this way. No, respectful and pure conduct in a situation of domestic violence demands that, when we are able, we remove ourselves from danger and seek help from all necessary authorities, including our local church pastors and elders, if they're willing. This is part of the good we must do in this circumstance, mindful of God and full of hope.

If we have any question about whether Peter sanctions abuse here, all we need to do is read the next verse in which Peter charges husbands, likewise, to follow in the steps of Jesus. Christian husbands must abstain from any passions of the flesh that would tempt them to use their power to belittle or to exploit. Rather than take advantage of women's comparative physical or social weakness in that culture—what I take Peter to mean by "the woman as the weaker vessel" (3:7)—Christian husbands show their wives honor and understanding. Peter leaves absolutely no room here for any sort of domineering. In Peter's day, for example, women generally weren't legal heirs. But despite distorted cultural messages about the value of one gender over the other, the Christian knows that believing men and believing women share full equality in their status as beloved sojourners, as coheirs of the grace of life. God takes the Christian husband's duty toward his wife so seriously that he will not hear his prayers if he abuses his authority.

For those Christian husbands who heeded Peter's instructions, consider how this would have made visible the grace of God among "the Gentiles" in that day. Consider how it would have shown forth the beauty of God's good design, in which a husband loves his wife as Christ loved the church and gave himself up for her. The winsome witness of a loving marriage has massive evangelistic power.

All of Life (3:8–12). Finally, in all of life, beloved sojourners resist evil and do good for the glory of God. As we relate to fellow believers, we abstain from things that divide us (3:8). We always bear in mind that we are siblings in Christ Jesus. So we have nothing to do with idle chatter that tears down, harshness of spirit toward one another, or arrogance. And as we relate to all people, we don't repay evil for evil or reviling for reviling, but we bless, "for to this you were called" (3:9). This is the same call—the call to walk in the steps of Christ (2:21). When, like Jesus, we bless the very person who persecutes us, we display our Christian identity in its most brilliant colors.

A dear friend of mine who is African American recently shared a story with me. His grandfather, Reverend Willie Jenkins Jr., raised his family in Pearl, Mississippi. Rev. Jenkins endured serious hardship since many politically and socially empowered people in his day mistreated him because of the color of his skin. Things grew especially tense in Pearl in the 1960s; families such as the Jenkinses, acting on the basis of their Christian conviction, worked toward ethnic integration in public schools. In response, a group of white teenagers habitually cruised through the Jenkinses' neighborhood, firebombing homes. One night, these white teenagers terrorized the neighborhood again. Rev. Jenkins and his young sons stood outside their house, ready to defend their family if need be. While the teenagers were engaging in their usual violence, the unexpected happened: they ran out of gas. Right in front of the Jenkinses' home. Before Rev. Jenkins stood a group of teenagers who repeatedly had victimized his family. His sons—stunned by the turn of events—looked up at their dad, ready to follow his command. He slowly left his post, picked up a glass bottle, and shattered it on the ground. His sons thought, "Here it comes!" To their great surprise, Rev. Jenkins then walked over to his car and started syphoning gasoline. His sons watched their father walk toward the white teenagers. With blood from the glass that had cut his skin and with gasoline running down his arm, he kneeled down and filled up the empty tank of his oppressors.

This is the way of the cross. It's a costly way but a blessed way. We know this way is blessed because we've seen how God the Father responded to his Son's way of life. He raised him from the dead, enthroned him at his right hand, and gave him rule over the entire cosmos (cf. Phil. 2:5–11).

God calls us to walk this Calvary road because he desires to bless us too: "that you may obtain a blessing" (1 Pet. 3:9). Peter teaches us this in 3:9–12 as he applies Psalm 34:12–16 to believers in Christ Jesus.[9] We obtain this blessing in part now, and we'll obtain it fully in the future. We're blessed now: "For the eyes of the Lord are on the righteous, and his ears are open to their prayer" (3:12). When we make visible God's goodness to a lost world, he is near, and his favor rests upon us. We know resurrection life in this world of suffering. And we'll be blessed in the future. Peter writes of seeing "good days" (3:10). When we lean upon the context of the whole letter, we understand the scope of these good days; and we will indeed see them. We will know resurrection life in the new heaven and the new earth—the place of our ultimate citizenship, where God will wipe away every tear and where he will reign in justice.

As we follow Christ in a death like his, so we shall follow him in a resurrection like his (cf. Rom. 6:5). Now we follow Jesus far from home, but one great and glorious day we shall follow Jesus home. Blessed be the God and Father of our Lord Jesus Christ!

Reflect and Pray

Reflect on each question and then take a moment to speak or write the prayers that grow from those reflections.

---

[9] 1 Pet. 2:11–3:12 may represent, in part, an extended meditation upon Psalm 34 and an application of it in light of the atoning work of Christ Jesus (cf. 1 Pet. 2:3).

1. At the center of this passage of commands are some verses about Jesus: 1 Peter 2:21–25. What different truths do we learn about Jesus in these verses? What difference do these verses make to the whole passage—and to you, personally?

2. How has a fellow believer shown you what it looks like to resist evil and do good for the glory of God, in one of the four contexts addressed in this passage? What did you learn from that example? In which of these four contexts might you pray to make progress in godly conduct for God's glory?

3. What phrases in this passage (2:11–3:12) make clear the purpose for which we should resist evil and do good? What are we beloved sojourners after, in the end? What kinds of prayers might these end goals lead you to pray?

Think Like an Expositor: Comments from Mary Willson

1. On the process of preparing to teach 1 Peter 2:11–3:12:

Active reliance upon God in prayer played the most important role in my preparation process. Staying focused on Peter's main idea and on his aim required discipline, and, by God's grace, I knew I needed his help for both. First, I needed God to keep me focused on Peter's main idea. As I pored over Peter's words and delighted in them, it was tempting to try to be thorough and share all the fascinating dynamics of this passage. I tried with God's help to prioritize what I saw as Peter's main idea and apply that to the hearts and lives of those I was teaching—which meant cutting a lot of content.

Second, I needed God to keep me focused on Peter's aim so that the goal and manner of my teaching would reflect the goal and manner of his instruction. In 1 Peter 2:11–3:12, Peter aims to help specific believers understand and live out their new identity in Christ, even in this unbelieving and unjust world. He is lovingly pastoring his flock with ethical instructions that are Christ-centered, gentle toward the weak, explicit in their evangelistic intent, sober-minded, full of hope, and specific to the life situations of his readers. So I asked God to help me follow Peter's lead. I posed this question to every major section of my exposition: Am I addressing God's people in their places of need, showing them concretely how their new identity in Christ transforms everything, and how God gives them what they need to live out this new identity for his glory and the good of their unbelieving neighbor? I prayed for specific people I knew I would be teaching, as well as for those I didn't know personally, asking God to minister his Word to their hearts.

2. On finding and communicating the unifying theme of the passage:

I finally articulated this passage's unifying theme (i.e., its central thrust or main message) in this way: As beloved sojourners, resist evil and do good for the glory of God! I wrestled with the passage's context and how it functions in the flow of Peter's pastoral exhortation to stand firm in true grace. I asked questions such as, "Were this passage to drop out of the epistle, what would be missing?" I also paid attention to repeated words such as "do/doing good," "be subject to," and "conduct" or "way of life"; these indicate that this is a passage about Christian ethics, that is, how we are to live out our new identity in this world. Just as the passage includes the indicative (i.e., what God has done for us) and the imperative (i.e., how we must live in response to what God has done for us), I wanted my unifying theme to have imperatival force ("resist evil and do good!") but be anchored in God's saving work in Christ ("as beloved sojourners").

Structurally, three elements influenced how I understood and expressed the unifying theme. First, Peter appears to distill his core principles in 2:11–12 and then to flesh them out in a variety of contexts in 2:13–3:12. So I grounded my unifying theme in 2:11–12 and found it developed in the rest of the passage. Second, I determined that 2:21–25 serves as the climax of the whole passage: here the principles of 2:11–12 culminate in the example of Jesus Christ, and here is the gospel anchor of the passage. Therefore I aimed for the climax of the passage to determine the climax of my exposition. For example, I applied the language of "beloved sojourner" to the Lord Jesus, identifying him as our perfect example and substitute according to the very language I chose for my unifying theme. Third, Peter in this passage repeatedly motivates his readers by the grace of God, calling them to hope in God and be assured of his blessing—especially poignant in his concluding citation of Psalm 34. I wanted to reflect that motivation and movement. Thus, the whole exposition flows: "far from home" to "following Jesus far from home" to "following Jesus home." This trajectory helped me convey the logic and pathos of Peter's exhortation.

3. On one aspect of this text that especially moved and challenged you:

I hardly know where to begin. When I considered how to illustrate each of my main points, I was profoundly encouraged as I remembered (and discovered) stories of our brothers and sisters in Christ throughout redemptive history who have embraced this cruciform way of life in the face of injustice, all by God's grace and for his glory. What a privilege to be family in Christ and to partner in the gospel together! Most of all, though, I was encouraged each time I meditated on the astounding humility and love of our Savior, the Lord Jesus, who "himself bore our sins in his body on the tree, that we might die to sin and live to righteousness. By his wounds you have been healed. For you were straying like sheep, but have now returned to the Shepherd and Overseer of your souls" (2:24–25). May the love of Christ compel me to lead a life of humble and loving servanthood, with great joy.

5

Sharing Christ's Sufferings, Showing His Glory

1 Peter 3:13–4:19

D. A. Carson

The passage assigned to me, 1 Peter 3:13–4:19, is a long one, but as it is important to follow the flow, I shall present it first in its entirety:[1]

> Who is going to harm you if you are eager to do good? But even if you should suffer for what is right, you are blessed. "Do not fear their threats; do not be frightened." But in your hearts revere Christ as Lord. Always be prepared to give an answer to everyone who asks you to give the reason for the hope that you have. But do this with gentleness and respect, keeping a clear conscience, so that those who speak maliciously against your good behavior in Christ may be ashamed of their slander.

---

[1] Unless otherwise noted, Scripture quotations in this chapter are taken from The Holy Bible, New International Version®, NIV®. Copyright © 1973, 1978, 1984, 2011 by Biblica, Inc.™ Used by permission. All rights reserved worldwide.

For it is better, if it is God's will, to suffer for doing good than for doing evil. For Christ also suffered once for sins, the righteous for the unrighteous, to bring you to God. He was put to death in the body but made alive in the Spirit. After being made alive, he went and made proclamation to the imprisoned spirits—to those who were disobedient long ago when God waited patiently in the days of Noah while the ark was being built. In it only a few people, eight in all, were saved through water, and this water symbolizes baptism that now saves you also—not the removal of dirt from the body but the pledge of a clear conscience toward God. It saves you by the resurrection of Jesus Christ, who has gone into heaven and is at God's right hand—with angels, authorities and powers in submission to him.

Therefore, since Christ suffered in his body, arm yourselves also with the same attitude, because whoever suffers in the body is done with sin. As a result, they do not live the rest of their earthly lives for evil human desires, but rather for the will of God. For you have spent enough time in the past doing what pagans choose to do—living in debauchery, lust, drunkenness, orgies, carousing and detestable idolatry. They are surprised that you do not join them in their reckless, wild living, and they heap abuse on you. But they will have to give account to him who is ready to judge the living and the dead. For this is the reason the gospel was preached even to those who are now dead, so that they might be judged according to human standards in regard to the body, but live according to God in regard to the spirit.

The end of all things is near. Therefore be alert and of sober mind so that you may pray. Above all, love each other deeply, because love covers over a multitude of sins. Offer hospitality to one another without grumbling. Each of you should use whatever gift you have received to serve others, as faithful stewards of God's grace in its various forms. If anyone speaks, they should do so as one who speaks the very words of God. If anyone serves, they should do so with the strength God provides, so that in all things God may be praised through

Jesus Christ. To him be the glory and the power forever and ever. Amen.

Dear friends, do not be surprised at the fiery ordeal that has come on you to test you, as though something strange were happening to you. But rejoice inasmuch as you participate in the sufferings of Christ, so that you may be overjoyed when his glory is revealed. If you are insulted because of the name of Christ, you are blessed, for the Spirit of glory and of God rests on you. If you suffer, it should not be as a murderer or thief or any other kind of criminal, or even as a meddler. However, if you suffer as a Christian, do not be ashamed, but praise God that you bear that name. For it is time for judgment to begin with God's household; and if it begins with us, what will the outcome be for those who do not obey the gospel of God? And, "If it is hard for the righteous to be saved, what will become of the ungodly and the sinner?"

So then, those who suffer according to God's will should commit themselves to their faithful Creator and continue to do good.

You can hit your thumb with a hammer; that will make you suffer. You can flunk an important exam; that will make you suffer. You can get jilted by your friend or spouse; that will make you suffer. You can die of leukemia at the age of fifteen; that will make not only you suffer but also all those around you. You can be bereaved after sixty years of marriage; that will make you suffer. You can have a stroke. You can fall off a horse. You can end up in a car accident; break a leg while skiing; slip and pour boiling water on your hand while you are cooking. You can writhe in the shame of remembered guilt. All these things will make you suffer. You can fuel the alienation and deep hurt of having been abused and maybe even become an abuser yourself. You can get tired, suffer a nervous breakdown, lose perspective, become nonfunctional. Shall I go on?

I am sure that many who read these pages have memories of a great deal of suffering. But, of course, the various categories of suffering that we experience or imagine are all alluded to at some point or another the Bible. I don't mean specific instances—I can't recall anybody banging his or her thumb with a hammer. But there is no broad category of suffering that has not been addressed in some fashion or other in Holy Writ.

This passage before us, 1 Peter 3:13–4:19, does not look at suffering on so broad a canvas. It focuses on distinctively Christian suffering—suffering that comes about for no other reason than that we are Christians, suffering that might take the form of insults and abuse and malicious condescension because we are Christians. In some parts of the world, it may result in a beating or in going to jail. Crucifixion has come back into vogue in some parts of the Middle East. Or perhaps you will face what happened to the missionary daughter of a friend of mine: you can serve in a corner of the world where you get gang-raped for Jesus's sake.

So I am focusing now primarily on the suffering that may come to us because we are Christians. That is what this passage is about. It will help to follow the flow of thought in the passage if we organize it into four sections—one long one and three shorter ones. In each case, there is an implicit or explicit command.

1. Do Not Withdraw, for Christ Is Your Example (3:13–22)

Peter has earlier hinted at the topic of persecution of Christians. He mentions it briefly in 1:6 and several times in chapter 2 and again in chapter 3. But now he treats it in an extended argument. He prepares the ground by saying that in many contexts Christians will *not* be harmed and should *not expect* to be harmed: "Who is going to harm you if you are eager to do good?" (3:13). He begins with this demurral because after Christians have faced some battering, they can become a little gun-shy. They may think of government only as an enemy. Instead of seeing, as Peter has made clear, that governments are ordained by God and designed to preserve order and to be honored by God's people—even a government led by Emperor Nero—such Christians are tempted to expect violence from their government even when it is not overtly threatened. In many ordinary facets of life, the government is not in any sense our enemy. We are called to obey civil authority, except in those instances where the government's mandate is in direct contradiction to the revealed will of God. The principle is clear enough: if you do not exceed the speed limit, you will not get a traffic fine. "Who is going to harm you if you are eager to do good?" (3:13). In other words, it is important to remember that ideally, and often in practice, authorities are set up to order life for the better, for human flourishing, for the good and security of the culture. In any case, they operate under God's providential sway (cf. Rom. 13:1–7).

On the other hand, "if you should suffer for what is right, you are blessed" (1 Pet. 3:14). This "blessing" alludes to the teaching of Jesus in the beatitudes. In Matthew 5 the last of the beatitudes is, "Blessed are those who are persecuted because of righteousness, for theirs is the kingdom of heaven" (v. 10). Blessed! As if that pronouncement is not enough, Jesus expands on that last beatitude, the only one he treats that way: "Blessed are you when people insult you, persecute you and falsely say all kinds of evil against you because of me. Rejoice and be glad, because great is your reward in heaven, for in the same way they persecuted the prophets who were before you" (vv. 11–12). So in that passage, those who are insulted or persecuted should see themselves blessed if the suffering they are enduring is "for righteousness' sake," or for the sake of Jesus's name. They should respond this way because (1) they are thereby aligning themselves with the prophets of God, and (2) they are aligning themselves with Jesus himself. That is the teaching of Jesus picked up here by Peter.

We must follow the flow from verse 14b to 15a: "But even if you should suffer for what is right, you are blessed. 'Do not fear their threats; do not be frightened.' But in your hearts revere Christ as Lord." Instead of withdrawing in fear, curbing our life and our witness so that we do not cause offense even if that offense is rooted in the gospel, this text says, "Don't fear their threats; don't be frightened; in your hearts continue to revere Christ as Lord." *Peter* is writing this—the Peter who in the past has known what it is to fear the threats of opponents. He cannot help but remember the night he sat in the courtyard and repeatedly swore that he didn't know who Jesus was, shamefully reduplicating his shame until the rooster crowed. Why did he act like that? Because he feared the authorities. He feared that he might be arrested. He feared what the servant girl thought of him. And he didn't revere Jesus Christ as Lord.

In fact, the thought of verse 14b is drawn from Isaiah 8. You may recall that Isaiah 8:14 is one of the "stone" passages quoted in chapter 2. Now the preceding verse from Isaiah 8 is picked up: "The LORD Almighty is the one you are to regard as holy," Isaiah says. "He is the one you are to fear, he is the one you are to dread" (Isa. 8:13). Peter paraphrases: "Do not fear their threats; do not be frightened" (1 Pet. 3:14b). What Peter tells his readers they must do, rather, is this: "In your hearts revere Christ as Lord" (1 Pet. 3:15a). We set Jesus Christ apart as holy and so confess his lordship in our thinking, in our responses, in our speech, in our choices, in our relationships. This, after all, is the Lord Jesus who uttered the words of Matthew 10:28: "Do not be afraid of those who kill the body but cannot kill the soul. Rather, be afraid of the One who can destroy both soul and body in hell." Christ has all authority. Indeed, that is the way 1 Peter 3 draws to a close: Christ "who has gone into heaven and is at God's right hand—with angels, authorities and powers in submission to him" (v. 22).

So, "always be prepared to give an answer to everyone who asks you to give the reason for the *hope* that you have" (3:15b). This theme of hope was already introduced back in chapter 1: "Praise be to the God and Father of our Lord Jesus Christ! In his great mercy, he has given us new birth into *a living hope* through the resurrection of Jesus Christ from the dead." That hope is an attitude of expectation, of longing, of attentive looking forward to what is coming—a living hope. Elsewhere Peter tells us that our hope is lodged in "a new heaven and a new earth, where righteousness dwells" (2 Pet. 3:13). We will unfailingly exult in the presence of God forever. All this we eagerly await, we "hope" for it, and this living hope we enjoy "through the resurrection of Jesus Christ from the dead" (1 Pet. 1:3). When it finally arrives, we will receive "an inheritance that can never perish, spoil or fade. This inheritance is kept in heaven for you" (1 Pet. 1:4).

As long as our entire horizon is filled with the activities, goals, and blessings of this life, how on earth will we find the nerve, the courage, or the vantage point to be able to stand up to persecution and say, "I can't go along with this wicked order because my citizenship is in the new heaven and the new earth. My hope is grounded in Christ Jesus. He has gone before me. He is my Lord. He has suffered death on my behalf. Already he enjoys resurrection existence, and one day I will share that with him. That is what I am eagerly looking forward to, and it shapes my values now"? Peter's point is that any thoughtful Christian can say that. It does not require a degree in apologetics; rather, it requires the willingness to give the reason for the hope that controls us. "Be prepared to give an answer to everyone who asks you to give the reason for the hope that you have."

Of course, such witness does not authorize us to be nasty. Peter carefully adds, "Do this with gentleness and respect"—not with smugness, condescension, or vicious anger, but "with gentleness and respect." After all, we are never more than poor beggars telling other poor beggars where there is bread. We conduct ourselves in this way, both so that we will keep a clear conscience and so that others, even if they disagree with us, cannot write us off as nasty hate-mongers: "keeping a clear conscience, so that those who speak maliciously against your good behavior in Christ may be ashamed of their slander. For it is better, if it is God's will, to suffer for doing good than for doing evil" (3:16–17).

I know a doctor in a North African country who has served for many years now in clinics that minister to Muslims. He has a quiet reputation for careful, godly, pleasant, effective witness. One of the stories about him that has filtered out is this: he was treating a woman who had a deep gash in her arm. As he worked, he explained how the wound had to be carefully cleaned to get rid of as many germs as possible so as to prevent infection. She listened, paused for a moment, and then commented, "It's not just my arm. I wish I had a clean heart." Now, what would you say? What would you say if you had a degree in Muslim apologetics? Might you be tempted to point out that the problem with Islam is that there is no atoning sacrifice that is offered to take away sin? That if you are accepted by Allah at the end, it's because you have obeyed him sufficiently for him to grant you a place in his presence? Christianity, by contrast, handles the dirt we have in our heart by providing a Savior to take it away. But this doctor personalized his response, testifying to his own *hope*. What he said was this: "Oh, I know just what you mean. I have had such a dirty heart myself, and then I met someone who took it all away. Would you like me to tell you about him?" With gentleness and respect, for conscience's sake, so that no one could rightly criticize him for being a triumphalist, he gently pointed her to Christ.

Especially as tensions rise in the culture and many of our attempts at "witness" turn into confrontations, it is easy to fantasize about contests where we have the last word, the smart answer, because we have studied deeply. Without for a moment undermining the value of deep study, our passage puts the focus elsewhere: "keeping a clear conscience, so that those who speak maliciously against your good behavior in Christ may be ashamed of their slander" (3:16).

"For it is better, if it is God's will, to suffer for doing good than for doing evil" (3:17). "If it is God's will" could refer to God's will that you suffer as opposed to the experience of other people who don't suffer. After all, in 3:13 we read of some people who don't suffer. Even in times of violent opposition, there are some people who are called to suffer and some people who aren't. Thus James becomes the first apostolic martyr, and Peter gets out of jail on an angelic pass (Acts 12). Peter is told what kind of death he will suffer in order to bring glory to Christ, and John is told that he might enjoy a very, very long life (John 21).

But if it is God's will, it is better "to suffer for doing good than for doing evil. For Christ also suffered once for sins, the righteous for the unrighteous, to bring you to God" (1 Pet. 3:17–18). He did not suffer for doing evil, but precisely to defeat evil—suffering, bearing our sins in his own body on the tree, the righteous for the unrighteousness (v. 18). *Thus, the exemplary nature of his cross work is grounded in the atoning work of his cross work.* Do not withdraw, for Christ is our example.

I must pause here to say that the verses that follow (3:18b–22) are amongst the most difficult in the New Testament to interpret. There are three main views and scores of variations. Let me tell you what the three principal interpretations are. I should confess to you that I'm not sure which one is right, but I'll defend the one that is, in my view, most likely, and show how it fits into the flow of the passage.

1. The first interpretation is that after Christ's death and before his resurrection, Jesus descends into hell and preaches to the spirits of those sinners who perished in the flood at the time of Noah. "He was put to death in the body but made alive in the Spirit. After being made alive, he went and made proclamation to the imprisoned spirits—to those who were disobedient long ago when God waited patiently in the days of Noah while the ark was being built" (3:18b–20). That's the first interpretation. In the early church, it was made famous by Origen.

2. The interpretation that I think is most likely to be correct was made popular by Augustine in the fourth century: Christ through the Spirit preached to the people who were alive in Noah's day. That is, Christ did not come in his incarnate form to the people in Noah's day, but through the Spirit he preached to the people who were alive in Noah's day. Then, subsequently, they died and faced judgment; they are now in prison, as it were, in hell, though they were not in hell when Jesus preached to them.

3. Another view says that the spirits in prison are fallen angels, not human beings, and what Jesus does, according to this passage, is descend into hell to preach to these fallen angelic spirits, the fallen angels, in order to declare his victory and their doom. That view is the most common one today.

There is no space to set out the pros and cons of each position. I shall restrict myself to providing some of the reasons why I understand this passage as I do and then show how this interpretation ties the passage to the context.

Begin with verse 18b: "He [Christ] was put to death in the body but made alive in the Spirit." Because those two expressions "in the body" and "in the Spirit" are parallel, this means that Christ was put to death in the domain of the body but made alive in the domain of the Spirit. The eternal Son of God did not have a body in eternity past, but the Word became flesh, he gained a body, and in the fullness of time he was put to death in that body. But he was made alive in the domain of the Spirit. That does not mean that in his post-resurrection existence he was ethereal, nonmaterial. After all, the apostle Paul in his great resurrection chapter, 1 Corinthians 15, can speak of the resurrection *body*, which could certainly be touched and handled and which was capable of eating and drinking, as a "spiritual body." By that, the apostle does not mean that Christ's resurrection body is so ethereal or nonmaterial that it could not be touched; rather, he means it is a body enlivened, transformed, from the domain of the Spirit. So Christ has been put to death in the flesh, in the domain of the body, and he has been made alive in this domain of the Spirit (3:18b).

Then, in the beginning of verse 19, there are several ways of translating what comes next. In this case I think the 2011 NIV, the translation I am using, is wrong and that the ESV has it right. The flow from verse 18b to verse 19 is best rendered, "He was put to death in the body but made alive in the Spirit through which [better: through whom] he went and made proclamation to the imprisoned spirits." That is, through this domain of the Spirit, he went and proclaimed something to these peoples. In fact, it was the domain of the Spirit that enabled him to speak to them. But that does not establish *when* he thus spoke to them.

We gain clarity when we remember two important passages in Peter's letters.

First, back in chapter 1 Peter writes, "Concerning this salvation, the [Old Testament] prophets, who spoke of the grace that was to come to you, searched intently and with the greatest care, trying to find out the time and circumstances to which *the Spirit of Christ in them* was pointing when he predicted the sufferings of the Messiah and the glories that would follow" (1:10–11). In other words, when Isaiah preached, it wasn't just Isaiah preaching. It was the Spirit of Christ in him, before Christ himself came into the world. When Ezekiel preached, it wasn't just Ezekiel preaching. It was the Spirit of Christ preaching through Ezekiel. And sometimes they themselves did not know how to put all these things together. They tried to figure out how the various prophecies that they were uttering would actually come together to be properly understood; and quite frankly, some of that understanding came only when Jesus himself showed up.

The best illustration, of course, is what takes place in Caesarea Philippi, in Matthew 16. There Peter says to Jesus, "You are the Messiah, the Son of the living God." Jesus approves Peter's confession: "Blessed are you, Simon son of Jonah, for this was not revealed to you by flesh and blood, but by my Father in heaven" (Matt. 16:16–17). But that doesn't mean that Peter understood by "Messiah" or "Christ" everything you and I understand by these words. You and I cannot confess Jesus as the Messiah without thinking of Jesus who died on the cross and rose again. We cannot avoid including Jesus's death and resurrection in our confession, because we live after those staggering events. But in Matthew 16 Peter doesn't incorporate those events into his confession. He believes that Jesus is the promised Davidic Messiah, but when Jesus goes on to talk about his impending death and how he must go to Jerusalem and be crucified and rise again on the third day, Peter turns on Jesus and says, "Never, Lord! This shall never happen to you!" (16:22). After all, messiahs win. They don't suffer and die; they triumph. But Jesus rounds on Peter and says, "Get behind me, Satan! You are a stumbling block to me; you do not have in mind the concerns of God, but merely human concerns" (16:23). So at one level, Peter proffered the right answer: Jesus is the Messiah, and that insight was given by God. And yet, at another level, Peter didn't have things put together. Even the apostles initially failed to understand that the promised Messiah would be the suffering servant. And according to 1 Peter 1, that was true of many Old Testament prophets. The prophets "spoke of the grace that was to come to you, [and they] searched intently and with the greatest care, trying to find out the time and circumstances to which the Spirit of Christ in them was pointing when he predicted the sufferings of the Messiah and the glories that would follow" (1:10–11). But that has now come by the gospel to you. So the Spirit of Christ was empowering the Old Testament prophets, was speaking through them, and as a result, they sometimes spoke better than they knew.

Second, in another important passage in Peter's writings, the apostle tells us that Noah in his day was a "preacher of righteousness" (2 Pet. 2:5). That is to say, he not only built a big boat, but he had countless years in which to preach and preach, warning against judgment to come and demanding repentance, and what he received in return was rejection and mockery. People did not believe.

What power impelled Noah to preach? Well, by the analogy of 1 Peter 1:11, he preached because the Spirit of Christ was in him, calling people of his day to repentance and faith. That brings us back to our primary passage in 1 Peter 3:19–20. We understand it to mean something like this: by the Spirit, Christ went and preached, at the time of Noah, to those who are now spirits in prison—spirits now in prison because they disobeyed formerly when God's patience was waiting in the days of Noah, when Christ was speaking through Noah, the preacher of righteousness. And as a result, they have ended up in hell. They were destroyed, and only eight people were saved. "God waited patiently in the days of Noah while the ark was being built," while repentance and faith were being preached—but "only a few people, eight in all, were saved through water, and this water symbolizes baptism that now saves you also" (vv. 20–21).

Peter sees that if Noah so preached, it was because of the Spirit of Christ who was in him. Doubtless we should ask ourselves why Peter draws this particular analogy. Why does his mind go to Noah? What insight does the story of Noah provide to his argument? Note the parallels between Noah's day and Peter's day. In Noah's day, there was a very small minority of people who believed the word of God and pursued righteousness, over against a broad culture that did not hear the word of God and did not receive it—very much as was the case in Peter's day. Noah was righteous in the midst of a wicked generation. He bore witness to those who were around him and was willing to be mocked for it, to be insulted for it, as Christians in Peter's day were called to bear witness to the truth of Christ and suffer for it and be mocked for it. In both cases, judgment was impending. Judgment was impending for Noah because the flood was on the horizon. Judgment was impending in Peter's day because, as we are told in the next chapter, "they will have to give account to him who is ready to judge the living and the dead" (1 Pet. 4:5). And in both cases, the righteous are finally saved, vindicated, approved by God.

This triggers in Peter's mind another parallel: Noah and his crew were saved through water—that is, not *from* water only, but *through* water. The very water that brought drowning and judgment also lifted the boat so that the water saved them. So Peter draws the obvious parallel—"saved through water, and this water symbolizes baptism that now saves you also" (3:20–21).

In what way does baptismal water save them? An illustration I sometimes use with my students at Trinity concerns Billy Sunday. At the end of the nineteenth century, he played baseball for the National League. Converted to Christ, during the first three decades of the twentieth century he became the most popular and influential evangelist in North America, frenetically preaching for repentance and faith, and against alcohol; many assert that he was instrumental in getting the Eighteenth Amendment adopted in 1919, introducing national Prohibition. It was his custom to put up a massive tent that could seat many thousands of people. When he invited people forward, it quickly became obvious that if he pitched his tent on the ground when it was dry, then people coming forward kicked up a lot of dust—and hacking and sneezing in the aisles are not conducive to piety. On the other hand, if he pitched his tent when the ground was wet, then when people come forward, the ground was inclined to turn to slush and muck, and the odd person would slip on it and fall down. And that was not conducive to piety either. So very soon he adopted the policy, soon followed by others, of putting down sawdust on all the aisles. Out of that simple practice came the expression, "hit the sawdust trail." To "hit the sawdust trail" became so common a way of talking about conversion to Jesus, becoming a Christian, getting born again, that the expression was picked up in the papers and magazines of the day. You could ask someone, "When did you become a Christian?" and he or she might reply, "Oh, I hit the sawdust trail in Cincinnati in '28." It might even be that somebody who had never been on a sawdust trail in his or her life would use that expression to refer to conversion. In other words, to "hit the sawdust trail" stood by metonymy (referring to something by naming an associated part of it) for conversion.

In the New Testament, baptism has many associations. But, in general, it is closely tied to conversion. So I suspect that when Paul writes that "all of you who were baptized into Christ have clothed yourselves with Christ" (Gal. 3:27), he is not talking about the power of the water. He is saying something akin to "all of you who were converted to Christ have clothed yourselves with Christ." In other words, he speaks about baptism in much the same way that people in Billy Sunday's days spoke about hitting the sawdust trail. In each case, the symbol stands by metonymy for the reality: "When were you converted?" "Oh, I was baptized in Corinth in 52" (although they used a different calendar then, so they wouldn't have said "52").

In other words, although "baptism" is a way of talking about a lot of things, the most important is conversion. In the first century, after Jesus had risen from the dead, if you became a Christian, you were converted, baptized, and joined to a local church as one act. It wasn't step one, step two, step three, separated by large expanses of time before you felt "ready" for the next step. The three were bound up together. It was impossible to think of a Christian who was unbaptized or a baptized Christian who was not a church member.

That is the way Peter uses "baptism" in our passage. The water was the means in the days of Noah by which Noah and his family were saved from destruction. And that "symbolizes baptism that now saves you." "Not [Peter immediately adds] the removal of dirt from the body but the pledge of a clear conscience toward God." The literal water might well wash off some literal dirt, but that is not what Peter has in mind when he talks about baptism. Rather, baptism stands by metonymy for your conversion in which you experience "the pledge of a clear conscience toward God," the initial stages of what it is like to live with a clear conscience in the presence of a holy God. For you know your sins have been paid for, and you stand just in God's eyes. All this and more is bound up with the symbolism of baptism associated with your conversion. So the conversion has saved you, represented by this baptism. "It saves you by the resurrection of Jesus Christ, who has gone into heaven and is at God's right hand—with angels, authorities and powers in submission to him" (3:21–22).

So now do you see the place of these difficult verses in the flow of the whole passage? Do not withdraw, for Christ is your example: (1) in his sufferings as an innocent victim; (2) in the constancy of his preaching through his Spirit, whether in Old Testament times or in present times; (3) in his final vindication—he has been vindicated by his heavenly Father. We, too, who press on in the faith and who refuse to withdraw from the conflict, will be vindicated on the last day.

So do not withdraw, for Christ is our example.

2. Do Not Be Sinful, for Christ Is Your Savior (4:1–6)

The willingness to suffer unjustly, as we've seen, follows the example of Christ. But the willingness to suffer is committed not only to bearing faithful witness but also to combating evil, even if this means suffering. "Therefore, since Christ suffered in his body, arm yourselves also with the same attitude, because whoever suffers in the body is *done with sin*" (4:1).

It is not always the case that the person who suffers in the body is more holy than the person who has not similarly suffered. Sometimes suffering makes people bitter, not better. Much suffering does not necessarily mean much holiness. Peter cannot help but know that. So why does he express himself as he does in verse 1? Peter assumes that if two people are following Christ, the one who does so in the teeth of physical suffering is making choices that reflect a counting of the cost and that decisively move a person away from easy believism, easy discipleship, into costly purity.

Quite a number of years ago, I knew a man in a church in England who had a privileged background. He was brought up in a Christian home with three older sisters. He was a nice kid, easy to please and readily accommodating. From the beginning of his life he replicated the Christian commitments well exemplified in his parents and in his three older sisters, the older sisters who doted on him. As a young man, he studied at the University of Edinburgh to become a medical doctor. He led the local campus ministry group. He married the right girl from the right Christian home. Those closest to him were happy with the directions he was taking. He eventually became a missionary in North Africa. Intrigued by public health medicine, he went to a leprosarium, and he and his wife served there for quite a number of years. When I first met him, he had left North Africa and moved to Cambridge, England, where he practiced medicine while pursuing specialist training in public health. Doubtless his missionary experience and his fair knowledge of Scripture assured that it wasn't long before he became an elder in the church. He proved particularly helpful when it came to men and women who had strange combinations of medical and spiritual ailments. He was known to be a reliable diagnostician, well able to provide good biblical advice and competent medical help.

And then out of the blue he announced that he was leaving his wife and two children and taking up with his nurse. No one saw it coming. We'll call him John. The pastor and others spoke with him. John's attitude at this time was, dominantly, "Why are you picking on me? I don't see that I'm doing anything wrong." To make a long story short, John divorced his wife and moved up north with his nurse, continuing his medical practice hundreds of miles from Cambridge, abandoning his wife and shattered daughters behind, and leaving the church to pick up the pieces.

About a year later, I was riding in a car with the pastor, heading to a conference. I asked him, "So what went wrong with John? What didn't we see? How do you explain what happened?" He replied, "Don, I'm convinced that John just wasn't a Christian." I said, "Come again? He was a missionary in North Africa, complete with leprosy, heat, flies, self-sacrifice. All of that Christian experience—not a Christian? He knew the creeds, he was a Christian leader, an elder in the church—what do you mean, not a Christian? On what basis do you say that?"

The pastor said, "I have gone over his life again and again, and I cannot find any significant place in his life where his faith cost him anything. He grew up as an eager-to-please kid, made a profession of faith, and was feted by his family. He became a doctor—oh, everybody cheered. He fell in love with a charming young woman. Everybody cheered again. Married her. Excellent. They went to Africa as missionaries—more approval. He served in a leprosarium—cheers for the self-sacrifice. When they returned to their country, they found a good church, and he was appointed an elder—more approbation. "At no point," said my friend the pastor, "can I find any place in his life where he made a decision to do something difficult, a decision taken not because he wanted to, but because it was right, a decision he didn't want to take because he knew that it was going to cost him something. He just went along, and at every point he did what he wanted to do, and he was cheered for his choices. And so when he found this pretty nurse, he did what he always did—he did what he wanted to do. And now he is the one who is surprised because nobody is cheering."

But if you are a genuine Christian, you want to do what is right even when there is much in you that would prefer to go another way. You want to please Christ, you want to identify with him, you want to speak boldly for him, you want to be aligned with him, even if all these choices are costly. You decide to make choices that cost you something. You trust Christ in the midst of illness and disappointment; you resolve to press on with faith and obedience and gratitude even when you watch friends die, when life's disappointments and hurts pile up. In short, those who have suffered in the flesh have made a break with sin.

Whoever suffers in the body in this sense is done with sin. "As a result, they do not live the rest of their earthly lives for evil human desires, but rather for the will of God. For you have spent enough time in the past doing what pagans choose to do—living in debauchery, lust, drunkenness, orgies, carousing and detestable idolatry. They are surprised that you do not join them in their reckless, wild living, and they heap abuse on you" (4:2–4). You, however, take the long view, for you are a Christian. "But they will have to give account to him who is ready to judge the living and the dead. For this is the reason the gospel was preached even to those who are now dead, so that they might be judged according to human standards in regard to the body, but live according to God in regard to the spirit" (4:5–6).

Christ came to save sinners; he came to destroy sin. Your discipleship means that you too are engaged in the battle against sin. Do not be sinful, for Christ is your Savior.

3. Do Not Be Half-Hearted, for Christ Is Your Coming Sovereign (4:7–11)

Peter now emphasizes the end: "The end of all things is near" (4:7). The end was alluded to, of course, in verse 5, where there is warning of judgment to come. Now it is explicit: "The end of all things is near." "Therefore," Peter exhorts us, "be alert and of sober mind" (4:7).

There are reasons for this exhortation: (1) so that we may pray unencumbered—"so that you may pray" (v. 7); (2) so that we may love profoundly (vv. 8–9), remembering that loving each other deeply is important because love covers over a multitude of sins. That includes practical love—offering hospitality to one another without grumbling (v. 9); (3) and not only so, but we are to deploy our gifts self-denyingly (v. 10), so if you are called to give away money, give it generously; if you are called to be a minister of the Word, don't forget that it is the word of God; if anyone speaks, he should do so as one who speaks the very words of God; and if your job is to serve, you should serve with all the strength that God provides. In other words, in every case, you deploy your gifts self-denyingly in the light of the end that is still to come.

The larger goal of these exhortations is "so that in all things God may be praised through Jesus Christ" (4:11). Almost as if the thought of such praise to God triggers adoration that cannot be suppressed, Peter bursts forth with a doxology: "To him be the glory and the power for ever and ever. Amen" (4:11).

This appeal has no power to anyone who is not a believer. To Christians, it is wonderfully comforting and spectacularly powerful: Do not be half-hearted, for Christ is your coming sovereign. Because of him, through him, we pant for the glory of God through Jesus Christ, and that vision dramatically transforms all the tasks and responsibilities to which we are called.

Do not be half-hearted, for Christ is your coming sovereign.

4. Do Not Be Afraid of Persecution, for Christ Is Your Pioneer, the One Who Has Gone Ahead (4:12–19)

I can do no more here than survey the flow of the argument.

1. *Persecution should never come as a surprise to Christians.* Biblically, historically, persecution is not uncommon. When it strikes, it might be awful; it will be hurtful; it could be horrific. But it should never come as a surprise. "Dear friends, do not be surprised at the fiery ordeal that has come on you to test you, as though something strange were happening to you" (4:12). The reason we should not be surprised, of course, is that we have a robust doctrine of sin. Believing the Bible as we do, we simply cannot believe that the world, all by itself, is getting better and better. We *expect* that there will be wars, genocide, rape, cruelty, sex slaves, bitterness and hate, arrogance, and fear of people coupled with no fear of God—and where such things prevail with special strength, there will also be persecution, which, after all, is merely one face of sin.

There have been many attempts in the last hundred years or so to give the impression that Western culture is getting better and better, and peace is just around the corner. That was the way many viewed Western culture before World War I—education, science, technology, and learning would quell wickedness and generate such goodness that there would be a cessation of hostilities and no more war. Then came World War I, the "war to end all wars," and after it was finally over, once again people hoped that with modern mechanisms of war, we had learned our lessons, and war would end. Then came World War II, along with genocide in the concentration camps and in the farms of Ukraine. And then came the Cold War and countless regional wars. And Vietnam. And an array of smaller wars in Africa. Yet after the Berlin Wall came down in 1989, some pundits started up again. In 1992 Francis Fukuyama, a Japanese-American scholar, wrote an interesting book with the title *The End of History and the Last Man*.[2] By this, he did not mean that history had literally come to an end. He meant that history as we know it—largely controlled by narratives of wars and struggles—comes to an end because the communist-capitalist divide is over and democracy is winning. It might take another three hundred years before skirmishes settle down, but we're basically moving toward worldwide democracy and worldwide peace. I remember reading the book and thinking to myself, "Either Jesus has it right, or you've got it right, but you're not both right." After all, Jesus says, "You will hear of wars and rumors of wars, but see to it that you are not alarmed. Such things must happen, but the end is still to come. . . . Then you will be handed over to be persecuted and put to death, and you will be hated by all nations because of me" (Matt. 24:6–9). In short, sin should always horrify us but never surprise us, and because sin is the seedbed of persecution, persecution may well horrify us but should never surprise us.

2. *Persecution should always serve as a cause of rejoicing for Christians, because it enables us to participate in the sufferings and the glory of Christ.* "Rejoice inasmuch as you participate in the sufferings of Christ, so that you may be overjoyed when his glory is revealed. If you are insulted because of the name of Christ, you are blessed, for the Spirit of glory and of God rests on you" (4:13–14). In other words, Christ's glory not only shines when he is vindicated at his resurrection and ascends to the right hand of the Father, and when he returns to reveal his matchless glory at the end of the age—but "the Spirit of glory and of God" also rests *on us* as we follow Jesus's pattern from the cross to the crown, from suffering to vindication, from persecution to glory. God's glory—his essential nature, his utter praiseworthiness—is displayed in the cross before it is displayed in the second advent. And similarly for us: "the Spirit of glory and of God" rests on us as we are insulted and persecuted

---

[2] Francis Fukuyama, *The End of History and the Last Man* (New York: Free Press, 1992).

on the way to the celestial city. In the case of Jesus, God's glory is displayed in Jesus's face as it shines with the brightness of the noonday sun, such that the angels cover their faces with their wings and cannot gaze upon him. But it was earlier displayed in the battered human being on a cross, a man with wounds and sweat and pain, suffering torture and agony as he bears the guilt of us, his image bearers, with his Father himself turning aside—that too is where his glory is revealed. That is why the early Christians spoke of Christ reigning from the cross—an idiotic notion to the Romans, but elementary Christianity to his followers.

So it cannot be too surprising if, as we follow the Lord Jesus, we trace out a similar trajectory. That is why Peter says, "If you are insulted because of the name of Christ, you are blessed, for the Spirit of glory and of God rests on you" (4:14). As the Spirit of glory and of God rested on Jesus when he was battered, so the Spirit of glory and of God rests on us when we are battered. That is why when the apostles were first beaten up, in Acts 5:41, Luke declares that they left "rejoicing because they had been counted worthy of suffering disgrace for the Name."

Suppose, in the next few years, it begins to cost something in this country to be a Christian. Suppose that for every insult, every slight, every smear in the press, every friend who turns his or her back on you because of your Christian witness—every time that happens, suppose you smile and thank God for the privilege of displaying the glory of Christ, rejoicing because you're counted worthy to suffer for the name. Won't that change the country in a hurry, and if not the country, at least the church? For indeed God declares, "It has been granted to you on behalf of Christ not only to believe in him, but also to suffer for him" (Phil. 1:29). "Not only so, but we also glory in our sufferings, because we know that suffering produces perseverance; perseverance, character; and character, hope" (Rom. 5:3–4). That is why the apostle Paul can write, "Now I rejoice in what I am suffering for you, and I fill up in my flesh what is still lacking in regard to Christ's afflictions"

(Col. 1:24). "Now if we are children, then we are heirs—heirs of God and co-heirs with Christ, if indeed we share in his sufferings in order that we may also share in his glory" (Rom. 8:17).

3. *Persecution should never come to us as the result of evil done by Christians*. That is why Peter immediately adds these words: "If you suffer, it should not be as a murderer or thief or any other kind of criminal, or even as a meddler" (1 Pet. 4:15). In other words, suffering imposed by the state or by the society is not always a sign of glory. It may be well-deserved justice. We are following the way of Jesus only if whatever persecution comes our way is not deserved. So-called persecution should never come to us as the result of evil done by Christians.

4. *Persecution always comes as a privilege for Christians*. Suffering that comes to us as just judgment is shrouded in shame. "However, if you suffer as a Christian, do not be ashamed, but praise God that you bear that name" (4:16).

5. *Persecution should sometimes be seen as a step in the purification of Christians*. The logic is straightforward: if judgment begins with us, what will the outcome be for unbelievers? "For it is time for judgment to begin with God's household" (4:17), with the church of Jesus Christ. This is the time, the age, when God, good heavenly Father that he is, metes out a measure of punishment on his people, invariably for their good. As James puts it elsewhere, "Consider it pure joy, my brothers and sisters, whenever you face trials of many kinds, because you know that the testing of your faith produces perseverance. Let perseverance finish its work so that you may be mature and complete, not lacking anything" (James 1:2–4). In other words, sufferings and trials play their part in making me a mature Christian—and what Christian does not want greater maturity? Show me the Christian who has suffered very little, and I'll show you an immature Christian. But Peter takes an extra step: if God's judgment "begins with us, what will the outcome be for those who do not obey the gospel of God?" (1 Pet. 4:17). When we face persecution, part of us should

be welling up in compassion for the persecutors, because they will face a greater judgment, an unrelenting judgment, one that issues not in purification but in destruction.

6. *Persecution should always be seen within the framework of God's faithful and providential rule over Christians.* "So then, those who suffer according to God's will should commit themselves to their faithful Creator and continue to do good" (4:19).

I conclude with a prayer:

> O Lord God, we do not want to romanticize suffering. But as we read of brothers and sisters in the church around the world who face much greater challenges in suffering for Christ's sake than we do, we hold them up in prayer before you now. We think of the perhaps two million who have suffered in the Sudan, of the Karen people in recent years in Burma, of those who have suffered on some of the Indonesian islands, of Nigerian brothers and sisters in Christ who suffer at the hands of the Fulani and of Boko Haram. We think of totalitarian regimes of various stripes, regimes that react, sometimes violently, to any claims of the sovereign Lord Jesus. We ask that somehow by your Spirit you will give your people in these places—how dare we ask it!—joy in their afflictions, steadfastness, glory, bearing witness because in their suffering they thus align themselves with King Jesus. And in our small corner, Lord God, where most of our suffering for the near future is likely to belong to the realm of insults and not much more, to minor legal difficulties, grant that instead of whining and asking where our inherited culture has gone, we may rejoice, because we too are beginning to be counted worthy to suffer for the name. We thank you for the privilege of filling up the sufferings of Christ in his body, the church. And we ask that we may do our share for Jesus's sake. Amen.

Reflect and Pray

Reflect on each question and then take a moment to speak or write the prayers that grow from those reflections.

1. This chapter's first summary point is: "Do not withdraw; Christ is your example." Look back through verses 13–17 of 1 Peter 3. What kinds of suffering are mentioned here? In what ways do we face such troubles today, and why might we be tempted to withdraw? What strikes you about the very different response commanded by Peter?

2. The person of Christ is obviously central to all the commands in 3:13–4:19. As you review this section of 1 Peter, list several of the truths about Jesus that emerge. How might each of these truths make a difference in your response to suffering?

3. In the last parts of his chapter Dr. Carson unfolds the joy and the benefits of suffering as a believer, according to 1 Peter 4. What characterizes the perspective of a Christian who rejoices in suffering? In what situations have you experienced or witnessed this kind of response to suffering?

Think Like an Expositor: Comments from D. A. Carson

1. On the process of preparing to teach 1 Peter 3:13–4:19:

Over the years I have preached through 1 Peter several times in different contexts and taught 1 Peter in Greek to numerous generations of seminary students. So I wasn't coming to this text "cold." When I was asked to handle this passage, I realized that my biggest challenge this time round was the length of the passage: what should I leave out? I decided to use the address to follow the flow of the entire section, and that was probably a mistake. I should have left out more, since the passage is both long and dense. So initially, then, my challenge was to provide an outline that followed the flow of this text (since I was already pretty familiar with the epistle) and figure out what to include and exclude. If I were asked to do it again, there would have been more exclusions.

2. On handling a passage with difficult and disputed meaning:

The first thing to do, of course, is try to understand the passage from your own study of it, following its logic and flow; Peter's use of words; the place of the passage in the context of the letter as a whole; working through a handful of good commentaries; and much more. In this case, one also finds embedded in the passage one of the most disputed and most difficult-to-understand texts in the New Testament, 3:19–22. At some point it is helpful to sort out what the options are (the best commentaries are helpful in this regard) and begin to reach some tentative conclusions. Granted how long the entire passage is, it simply isn't possible to go through the major options and show your reasoning to the congregation. That may be a good step to take if the entire address is restricted to these disputed verses, but in my case I could not do more than warn people that the meaning of these verses is debated, provide my tentative understanding of the passage, and tease out some of its implications.

3. On one aspect of this text that especially moved and challenged you:

Probably the most striking challenge in the text is the comprehensive antithesis Peter draws between those who are genuinely believers and those who have not been redeemed. This not only bears on our attitudes toward suffering (which, after all, surfaces throughout the entire letter, and not just in this passage), but touches the use of our tongues, fighting off sin (spelled out pretty graphically in 4:3b), the primacy of loving other believers and showing hospitality, the ways in which we should discharge our varied responsibilities, and the sheer joy of being identified with Christ (not least in his sufferings) and of awaiting without fear the consummation to come. In other words, we Christians are not, in Peter's mind, just like the rest of the world but with a little something extra, but radically different from the world.

6

A Shepherd and a Lion

1 Peter 5:1–14

John Piper

Woven through the entire letter of 1 Peter is the repeated call for a condition of heart, and a way of life, that makes sense only if we are absolutely sure we will have a great reward in heaven. Peter calls believers again and again to think and feel and act in a way that can be explained only by an unshakable, all-satisfying hope beyond this life.

Of course, I don't mean the hope for material wealth, or pain-free health, or reunion with loved ones, or perfect leisure, or futility-free productivity in the age to come—all of that is true, but not central or primary. The ultimate reward that makes sense of the life Peter calls us to live is the reward of being with God and enjoying his beauty.

This is the main thing Jesus died for. And this alone can make sense of the counterintuitive life Peter calls us to live. In 1 Peter 3:18— one of the most important verses in the Bible, I think—Peter says,

"Christ . . . suffered once for sins, the righteous for the unrighteous, *that he might bring us to God.*" This is why he died for us, "that he might bring us to God." Not for punishment but for pleasure.

In your presence there is fullness of joy;
   at your right hand are pleasures forevermore. (Ps. 16:11)

That is what Christ died for. That is our final reward. That is our ultimate hope. All else is overflow and secondary. If you don't want God as your supreme satisfaction, then you don't want heaven, and you don't want what Jesus died to give.

But if you do—if Jesus is your inexpressible joy, as 1 Peter 1:8 says—then this letter will make sense to you, and the way of life Peter calls for will be possible. This is a mind-set and a way of life that can be explained only by an unshakable, all-satisfying hope beyond this life.

The Only Explanation Is Hope

Have you ever been troubled by 1 Peter 3:15 the way I have? "Always [be] prepared to make a defense to anyone who asks you for a reason for the hope that is in you." Why would people ask that question? Why would they look at our lives and ask about hope? Because the life Peter is calling for can be explained only by a hope that the world does not know. Following are four examples.

1. In 1 Peter 1:6–7, Peter calls us to rejoice in suffering. What makes sense of that? Hope beyond this life! ". . . so that the tested genuineness of your faith—more precious than gold that perishes though it is tested by fire—may be found to result in praise and glory and honor at the revelation of Jesus Christ." Note the incomparable reward of glory and honor at the coming of Christ.

2. In 1 Peter 3:5–6, Peter calls Christian wives to "do good and do not fear anything that is frightening." What makes sense of that? This is how the holy women who *hoped in God* used to adorn themselves. The Christ-exalting

fearlessness of a Christian woman is explained only by hope that goes beyond this world—hope in God.

3. In 1 Peter 3:9, Peter commands us, "Do not repay evil for evil or reviling for reviling, but on the contrary, bless." What makes sense of that? The hope of everlasting blessing. Because "to this you were called, *that you may obtain a blessing.*" Returning good for evil, when it may cost us our lives in this world, is possible because we put our hope in a blessing beyond this world.

4. In 1 Peter 4:13, Peter calls for counterintuitive behavior: "Rejoice insofar as you share Christ's sufferings." What makes sense of that? The goal is "that you may also rejoice and be glad when his glory is revealed."

So I say again that woven through this entire letter is Peter's repeated call to think and feel and act in a way that can be explained only by an unshakable, all-satisfying hope beyond this life, the hope of being with God, seeing and sharing his glory.

Suffer and Serve

And what is that peculiar way of thinking and feeling and acting that makes sense only in the light of hope beyond the grave? It is *a joyful, humble willingness to suffer wrong and serve rather than return evil for evil.*

- "What credit is it if, when you sin and are beaten for it, you endure? But if when you do good and suffer for it you endure, this is a gracious thing in the sight of God." (1 Pet. 2:20)
- "Even if you should suffer for righteousness' sake, you will be blessed." (1 Pet. 3:14)
- "It is better to suffer for doing good, if that should be God's will, than for doing evil." (1 Pet. 3:17)
- "Since therefore Christ suffered in the flesh, arm yourselves with the same way of thinking." (1 Pet. 4:1)
- "Let those who suffer according to God's will entrust their souls to a faithful Creator while doing good." (1 Pet. 4:19)

This is the strange, counterintuitive way of life Peter calls for that causes people to ask a reason for the hope that is in us: *a joyful, humble willingness to suffer wrong and serve, rather than return evil for evil.* Another name for this is *love.*

An Otherworldly Mind-Set

So when we come now to the final chapter of 1 Peter, this otherworldly mind-set and this otherworldly hope are the two threads woven through Peter's final thoughts. First, a quick overview to see that this is so. And then we will walk more slowly through the text and look more closely.

Humble Leadership (5:1–4)

In verse 1 of chapter 5, Peter presents himself not as an apostle, as in 1:1, but as a fellow elder alongside the elders in the churches: "So I exhort the elders among you, as a fellow elder."

This is a humble thing to do. He is modeling the humility and joyful readiness to serve that he is about to call for. It's rooted in the fact that he has seen Christ suffer and serve like this, and he is expectant that he is going to share in the coming glory. "I exhort . . . you, as . . . a witness of the sufferings of Christ, as well as a partaker in the glory that is going to be revealed" (v. 1b).

Then he calls for that kind of service from the elders in verses 2b–3:

> Verse 2a: "not under compulsion, but willingly, as God would have you";
> Verse 2b: "not for shameful gain, but eagerly";
> Verse 3: "not domineering over those in your charge, but being examples to the flock."

How does this make sense in a world where the very stuff of leadership is coercion and money and power? The answer lies in verse 4: "When the chief Shepherd appears, you will receive the unfading crown of glory." Hope beyond this life—that is why it makes sense.

This way of sacrificial, joyful, humble leadership makes sense *because of the hope of glory at the coming of Christ.* "You will receive the unfading crown of glory." The life of true biblical eldership makes sense only in the light of eternity. If it is explainable in natural terms, something is defective.

Lowliness and Servanthood (5:5–7)

Then in verses 5–7, Peter takes that same mind-set and applies it to all of us. You see that in the word "likewise" at the beginning of verse 5: "Likewise"—that is, just as the elders are called to be humble and serve you as examples rather than lording it over you—"you who are younger, be subject to the elders. Clothe yourselves, all of you, with humility toward one another."

How can that make sense in a world where humility and lowliness and servanthood do not get you a political nomination and do not get you a job—a world where self-promotion and self-exaltation are woven into the fabric of Roman and American culture? The answer lies in verses 5b–6: It makes sense because "God opposes the proud but gives grace to the humble."

What grace? Don't we already have grace? Yes, we do. But there is a future grace—more grace—coming to believers who clothe themselves with humility toward each other: "Humble yourselves, therefore, under the mighty hand of God *so that at the proper time he may exalt you*" (v. 6). This is why such a strange, humble, self-effacing attitude, one that is willing to suffer and serve rather than return evil for evil, makes sense. It makes sense because just over the horizon of this world, all the lowly nobodies who suffered in obedience to Christ will shine like the sun in the kingdom of their Father (Matt. 13:43).

Think of it. There are hundreds of thousands of faithful Christians around the world in very difficult circumstances, and while they joyfully endure the hardships of following Christ, only a handful of people even know they exist.

There is going to be a great reversal. It is only a matter of time. Followers of Jesus do not need the reward of this world. We don't need to be treated well. We don't need to prosper. Like those elders in verses 2 and 3, we don't need to be coerced in order to serve gladly. We don't need riches to be happy in the ministry. We don't need power in order to feel a sense of significance, because we have set our hope not on the exaltation of this world but on the exaltation and glory of the next. And there is no comparison.

The Lion Who Devours (5:8–10)

In verses 8–10, Peter tells us how to deal with the roaring lion of the Devil, who wants to devour us:

> Be sober-minded; be watchful. Your adversary the devil prowls around like a roaring lion, seeking someone to devour. Resist him, firm in your faith, knowing that the same kinds of suffering are being experienced by your brotherhood throughout the world. And after you have suffered a little while, the God of all grace, who has called you to his eternal glory in Christ, will himself restore, confirm, strengthen, and establish you.

The Devil here is not pictured as a sly snake who sneaks up on you and bites your heel. He is a roaring lion. Why roaring? Lions roar when they are hungry and angry. This Devil is not trying to sneak up on you. He is trying to terrify you, make you afraid, fill you with anxieties, and keep you off-balance and nervous.

How does this roaring lion devour people? Verse 9b explains: ". . . knowing that the same kinds of suffering are being experienced by your brotherhood throughout the world." This lion is roaring and biting and clawing by causing people—Christians in particular—to suffer.

His aim is to destroy Christians through suffering. He aims to make us doubt the goodness of God or the presence of God or the power of God or the compassion of God. This is how the horrible roar works. The claws. The teeth.

And Peter tells us, "Resist him, firm in your faith" (v. 9a). This does not mean that if you are successful, the claws never cut and the teeth never sink in. It means, when the claws cut and when the teeth sink in, don't stop believing! Don't stop being humble. Don't stop returning good for evil. Don't stop rejoicing. Don't stop loving. That is successful resistance to the roaring lion, even if it costs you your life.

Really? Keep on returning good for evil? When the adversaries are agents of the Devil? When they go on reviling and threatening us? Really? Keep on blessing? Keep on doing good? What could make sense out of that response to the lion? The answer comes in verse 10: "After you have suffered a little while, the God of all grace, who has called you to his *eternal glory* in Christ, will himself restore, confirm, strengthen, and establish you."

Resist the lion with unwavering joy and humility and love. Keep on doing good to those who hate you. How? By believing verse 10 with all your heart. Keep on hoping in this—this eternal glory, this promise of total restoration and confirmation and strength everlasting, unshakable, established glory. This future beyond the suffering of this world—*that* is the key.

Future Hope Endures Present Trouble

So, to the elders (vv. 2–3): don't lord it over your people. Don't use them for money. Don't begrudge their needs. Serve them eagerly, willingly, joyfully, humbly. How? In the rock-solid hope that "when the chief Shepherd appears, you will receive the unfading crown of glory" (v. 4).

To all of us (vv. 5–7): "Clothe yourselves, all of you, with humility toward one another. . . . Humble yourselves, therefore, under the mighty hand of God." How? In the hope that "at the proper time he may exalt you" (v. 6b).

And to the sufferers (vv. 8–10): resist this roaring lion in his power to attack with suffering. How? In the rock-solid hope that "after you have suffered . . . the God of all grace, who has called you to his eternal glory in Christ, will himself restore, confirm, strengthen, and establish you" (v. 10). Everything good you have lost will be restored in that glorious day.

Woven through this entire letter of 1 Peter, including chapter 5, is the call for a condition of heart and a way of life that make sense only if we are absolutely sure we will have a great reward in heaven.

That condition of heart and the way of life are *a joyful, humble willingness to suffer wrong and serve rather than return evil for evil.*

And that reward in heaven is *a crown of glory and exaltation in the presence of the all-satisfying God.* All wrongs against us will be set right. All patience under mockery will be vindicated. All shame in this world will be taken away and replaced with honor. All pain will be removed and all losses restored. All brokenness will be mended. All humiliation will be exchanged for garments of glory. All slander will be revealed as false before the whole world. All anonymity in quiet faithfulness will be replaced with global fame among the millions of the redeemed.

In this letter, God calls us to a kind of heart and a kind of life that makes no sense in this world—joyful, humble willingness to suffer wrong and serve rather than return evil for evil. It makes sense only if we are sustained by the hope of glory.

Your Motive and the Devil's Authority

All this leaves us with at least two questions: (1) How can it be loving to be motivated by your own desire for vindication and glorification? Why isn't that selfishness? (2) Is the Devil really in charge of suffering? When we suffer, is it simply the Devil roaring and clawing and biting? What about God? What's he doing when the Devil roars?

First, how can it be loving to be motivated by your own desire for vindication and glorification? Why isn't that selfishness? Listen again to 1 Peter 3:9: "Do not repay evil for evil or reviling for reviling, but on the contrary, bless, for to this you were called, *that you may obtain a blessing.*" And 1 Peter 5:6: "Humble yourselves, therefore, under the mighty hand of God *so that at the proper time he may exalt you.*"

Peter motivates us to humble ourselves and to bless our enemies by saying, "so that he may exalt you"—that you may obtain a blessing. Why is this not selfishness? How can this be love? I'll give five reasons, and as we move from one to five, they become increasingly decisive.

1. In the age to come, we will not exalt ourselves. We leave it totally in the hands of God whether he will be pleased to give us that reward.
2. When the reward comes, it will be all of "grace," not merit. "God opposes the proud but gives *grace* to the humble" (1 Pet. 5:5). God is not paying us a debt. God owes us nothing. It will all be free grace.
3. The exaltation and the glory we want is not *over* anyone else (unlike James and John when they asked for the highest places over the other apostles). It is an exaltation and a glory *out* of our misery—out of being maligned and slandered and persecuted. It is vindication that our message has been true. The aim is not to say, "I told you so," with a sneer. The aim is the establishment of the truth. What we have spoken is true and glorious.

These last two are decisive:

4. There is nothing morally inferior or defective about wanting reward for our behavior, provided that the reward is ultimately *more of Christ as the supreme joy of our souls*. The reason that is not morally inferior but is, in fact, a great virtue is that Christ is most glorified in us when we are most satisfied in Christ. It is no virtue—and no honor to Christ—to say, *I am going to suffer for Christ, and it makes no difference to me whether it leads to knowing and enjoying Christ better*. That is not a virtue. That is self-sufficiency cloaked as sacrifice.
5. Finally, it is *loving* to sacrifice for others with a view to reward, *if* our aim is that in the sacrifice, we would win others to come with us into the reward. First Peter 2:12 is critical: "Keep your conduct among the Gentiles honorable, so that when they speak against you as evildoers,

they may see your good deeds and glorify God on the day of visitation."

Our motive in returning good for evil is never that we get the reward and they don't. Our aim is always: I am joyfully willing to suffer in doing good to you as you do me harm so that you might see how satisfying my God is and be drawn with me into the reward of my sacrifice.

The aim of Christian suffering with joy is to show the all-surpassing value of Christ and to win as many people as possible with whom to enter into his all-satisfying glory. Grace is not a zero-sum game, as if there is a limited amount, so that if I get some, you get less. It's the opposite. Your sharing in it through my service *enlarges mine*. A shared joy is a doubled joy!

So when Peter over and over again motivates sacrifice by the promise of eternal glory, he is *not ruining* love; he is making it *possible*. He's *empowering* it.

Now our last question: Is the Devil really in charge of suffering? When we suffer, is it simply the Devil roaring and clawing and biting? What about God? What's he doing when the Devil roars?

Peter writes, "Resist [the devil], firm in your faith, knowing that the same kinds of suffering are being experienced by your brotherhood throughout the world" (1 Pet. 5:9). It's plain that Peter means that Satan is causing this suffering. Suffering is Satan's roar. This is exactly what Jesus said in Revelation 2:10 to the church in Smyrna: "Do not fear what you are about to suffer. Behold, the devil is about to throw some of you into prison, that you may be tested, and for ten days you will have tribulation. Be faithful unto death, and I will give you the crown of life."

So Satan can throw you in prison and keep you there until you die. And Peter would add that after you have suffered in prison and died, "the God of all grace, who has called you to his eternal glory in Christ, will himself restore, confirm, strengthen, and establish you" (1 Pet. 5:10). So don't give up your faith.

Trust him unto death. You will be raised from the dead. You will be glorious.

But that's not the whole story, is it? We know it's not. Satan is not the ultimate authority behind our suffering. Satan caused Job's suffering, but he had to get God's permission to do it (Job 1:12; 2:6–7). And Job saw the plan of God behind Satan: "'Shall we receive good from God, and shall we not receive evil?' In all this Job did not sin with his lips" (Job 2:10). Peter has the same theology of God's sovereignty in our suffering:

> "Therefore let those who *suffer according to God's will* entrust their souls to a faithful Creator while doing good." (1 Pet. 4:19)
>
> "It is better to suffer for doing good, *if that should be God's will*, than for doing evil." (1 Pet. 3:17)
>
> "In this [hope] you rejoice, though now for a little while, *if necessary*, you have been grieved by various trials [necessary for what?], so that the tested genuineness of your faith—more precious than gold that perishes though it is tested by fire—may be found to result in praise and glory and honor at the revelation of Jesus Christ." (1 Pet. 1:6–7)

Yes, Satan roars in our suffering. And his roar is all the louder because he knows he cannot act on his own. He can do no more harm to God's people than God designs for the refining of the gold of their faith. He roars with anger and frustration that his evil aim to punish God's elect ends up purifying their faith—the very thing he wants to destroy!

He Will Not Fail You

So I don't conclude with a simple formula for when to accept being slandered and when to confront it; when to turn the other cheek; when to endure mistreatment as a believer, and when to rebuke and admonish; when to spank a child, and when to be lenient; when to confront your husband about a shortcoming, or when to forbear; when to endure discrimination against yourself for your faith at work, and when to plead for justice; when to move to a dangerous place for Christ's sake, and when to leave a place because of danger.

Instead of a formula, I conclude with the resounding message of 1 Peter: that you think and feel and act in a way that makes sense only if you are absolutely sure that we will have a great reward in heaven—a way of life that can be explained only by an unshakable, all-satisfying hope beyond this life. It is a way of life, as 1 Peter 3:15 says, that will cause people to ask about the hope that is in you: a joyful, humble willingness to suffer wrong and serve rather than return evil for evil.

You know—through the death and resurrection of Christ, God has made you know—that a crown of glory awaits you. You will be exalted at the right time. "God . . . has called you to his eternal glory in Christ," and, after you have suffered, he "will himself restore, confirm, strengthen, and establish you" (1 Pet. 5:10).

You know he will because 1 Peter 5:7 says, "[Cast] all your anxieties on him, because he cares for you." And in verse 11, he says, "To him be the dominion forever and ever."

Total care and absolute dominion—he will not fail you. He cannot fail you. The glory of your future is absolutely certain. This is the grace of God! Stand firm in it (1 Pet. 5:12).

Reflect and Pray

Reflect on each question, and then take a moment to speak or write the prayers that grow from those reflections.

1. Reread Dr. Piper's opening paragraph, about Peter's call to believers to set their hope on reward beyond this life. Why are we often so slow to follow this call? How has the epistle of 1 Peter helped you to grasp the hope of your inheritance in Christ?

2. Peter calls leaders and all of us to humility. Why is this humility right and good, according to 1 Peter 5? In what ways is this humility utterly countercultural? How can a Christian cultivate such humility?

3. We end the book of 1 Peter with a lion on the prowl but the grace of God abounding to the end. In what ways does 1 Peter 5:10 encourage you to stand firm in the true grace of God? Write a final prayer, incorporating this verse into your words of praise and petition.

Think Like an Expositor: Comments from John Piper

1. On the process of preparing to teach 1 Peter 5:

In this particular case, I memorized the chapter. I had done that years before, so it was not as time-consuming as it might have been otherwise. I did this partly so that I would have a good grasp of the whole, and partly so that I could model for the women at the conference how important I think Scripture memory is—and that even old people can do it! I also think Scripture has an unusual power when spoken to others eye to eye and mouth to ear, reciting it, rather than eye to page, simply reading.

The most crucial thing in my preparation was to see how chapter 5 was part of Peter's primary emphasis on a way of life that can be enabled and explained only by the certainty of great reward in heaven—namely, a joyful, humble willingness to suffer wrong and serve rather than return evil for evil. I thought it was crucial that this theme be drawn out of chapter 5 and that the several motives of reward be made explicit—the crown (v. 4), more grace (v. 5), exaltation (v. 6), restoration, confirmation, strengthening, and establishment (v. 10).

One more thing: good teaching asks questions that may not seem readily obvious at first glance but prove to be important in real life. So I posed the question: How can it be loving to others if we are motivated to love them by a reward for ourselves? I think this kind of question, which does not lie on the surface of the text but begs to be answered just below the surface, tends to make people wake up and listen.

2. On training ourselves to discern and delight in the God-centeredness of such a passage:

One of the crucial parts of training our minds to see God-centered reality is to settle the question, What is the ultimate joy and the ultimate evil of life? What is the joy that makes all joys good joys rather than God-competing joys? What is the evil that makes all evils ultimately evil—evil in the eyes of God?

My answer to the first question is that God himself is our ultimate joy, and all other joys are joys because they give us something of God. If they don't, they are evil joys and draw the heart away from God. My answer to the second question is that the ultimate evil is preferring anything more than God. This is what made Adam's and Eve's first sin evil. It is what Jeremiah calls evil in Jeremiah 2:13, and it is what Paul described in Romans 1:20–23 as the universal sin of man.

If you think your way to the bottom of joy and evil in this way, then every text that touches on joy or evil touches on God. Every text that touches on what is good or evil, joy or sorrow, deals ultimately with God. In this way, virtually every text that touches on what matters to us leads us to God.

3. On one aspect of this text that especially moved and challenged you:

Few texts in all the Bible are as precious as the promise from the Creator of the universe that he cares for me. To believe this with all my heart is the great challenge of my life. Of course, I do not deserve this, and so Jesus's blood is the key to my hope that it could be so. But it is so! He says it! "He cares for you" (v. 7). But Peter says that the great challenge is not whether I feel worthy of that care but whether I am humble enough to receive it. "Humble yourselves . . . casting all your anxieties on him, because he cares for you" (1 Pet. 5:6–7). That is the great challenge: Am I humble enough to receive the all-supplying care of God?

Conclusion

Help Me Teach 1 Peter

Nancy Guthrie and John Piper

The following is drawn from the transcript of a live recording of an interview with John Piper by Nancy Guthrie for the "Help Me Teach the Bible" podcast, conducted on June 17, 2016, at the Gospel Coalition Women's Conference in Indianapolis, Indiana. In an effort to reflect the actual conversation, we have kept our edits to a minimum except where needed for clarity. Complete unedited audio of the interview is available at http://resources.thegospelcoalition .org/library/help-me-teach-1-peter-with-john-piper.

Nancy Guthrie: There are lots of things we can pick up and teach. Sometimes as teachers we look for a popular book that we think people will want to discuss, a topical book. And honestly sometimes we think to ourselves that maybe more people will come and be more interested in what we're offering if it's some popular book that's been on the best-seller list or one everybody's been talking about, rather than actually picking a book of the Bible to open up and teach—whether in our home, to the youth group, the women's Bible study, or a Sunday school class. So why should we be interested in equipping ourselves to open up a book of the Bible and preparing ourselves to teach that book?

John Piper: Well, I don't have any categories in my brain for relating to people who don't think it's interesting when God talks. If they want to read a John Piper book instead of the Bible, they're crazy. That sort of attitude really is, I think, a matter of unbelief that "all Scripture is breathed out by God and profitable for teaching, for reproof, for correction, and for training in righteousness, that the man [or woman] of God may be complete, equipped for every good work" (2 Tim. 3:16–17). That's a lot of works! Do you want to be equipped for every good work at home, every good work in the neighborhood, every good work at church, every good work at work? Read your Bible, study your Bible, and know your Bible through and through. It can't get more important than when God talks. And it's interesting when he talks. It's not just important and life changing; God is endlessly insightful and fascinating. We've just hardened ourselves with platitudes against the amazing things that are here in the Bible.

Nancy Guthrie: So you've made a case for why you would want to teach from the Bible. Why might I want to choose the book of 1 Peter to teach?

John Piper: Well, because you might lose your job if you say you think so-called gay marriage doesn't exist (which is what I would say), or that you think homosexual behavior (not orientation) might result in a person's destruction. That's what 1 Peter is about. So it's relevant because the world we live in is increasingly like the world into which Peter wrote this letter. I think it is perpetually relevant, because the John Piper that I want to be is the John Piper of this book. I'm not there yet. When I read about the kind of person Peter is calling us to be in all these relationships—citizen relationships, work relationships, marriage relationships, church relationships—and look at myself in comparison to the ideal he holds up of being an incredibly humble, tenderhearted, brotherly, returning-good-for-evil, slow-to-anger person, I just shake my head and say, "I need 1 Peter. I really need 1 Peter." I taught it a year ago in the fall of 2015 at Bethlehem College & Seminary to a group of sixteen or seventeen guys working in the Greek text. I chose it because of all those things I just said. Culturally and personally it's a riveting book for me.

Nancy Guthrie: So many of the Epistles come from the pen of Paul. And when we read them, we think about his history of being a "Hebrew of Hebrews" (Phil. 3:5) but also having been a persecutor of Christians. We hear a bit of his personality in his letters. We have just 1 and 2 Peter from Peter. So how does what we know about Peter from what we read in the Gospels, as well as what we read about him in Acts, inform our teaching? As we begin to teach this book, how do we set the stage regarding who Peter is? Do we just let that arise in the text? I'm thinking about our first week, and the first word of the book is "Peter."

John Piper: I'm a really bad example if it comes to stage-setting secondary things. So let me answer with a qualified no, I don't spend a lot of time setting the stage by looking at other texts about Peter first. And here's the reason: I really want this book to tell me who Peter is. I really want this book to set the agenda about what Peter thinks is important to know about Peter. I might bring something from a story about Peter that Peter would say is going to be misleading in terms of this book.

I think a lot of people come to the Bible thinking they've got to know first-century culture to teach it. Cappadocia, Bithynia, Asia—where are they? Who cares? Let 1 Peter tell you whether that's important. There will be clues, won't there? Is the setting of those Roman provinces in Asia Minor important? Let 1 Peter tell you whether or not they're important. Frankly, I think it would make a colossally boring first session to put up a map and work that over. You've probably done that; I've done it. I get done doing it and realize they're going home with a little geography in their head but their marriage stays the same, their kids stay the same, pride stays the same, everything stays the same. You can teach a very faithful and powerful series on 1 Peter without being an expert on first-century geography or Roman culture or exactly what the persecution was. Commentaries write whole introductions on what the persecution was. I say, just read it and see what Peter wants to tell you about the persecution. I think that's the most faithful and safe way, because if you start bringing stuff in from outside, you might bring stuff in that he doesn't want brought in.

Nancy Guthrie: So as you taught through 1 Peter last year, you broke this five-chapter book into fourteen sessions.

John Piper: I need a lot more.

Nancy Guthrie: Don't we always have to keep figuring out what we're going to cut out? Oftentimes that is part of the job of a Bible teacher. Why do you say you need a lot more time?

John Piper: Because I don't lecture. If I lectured, I could control totally how long this lasts. We could fit it in to the minute and cover everything perfectly. That's not a good way to teach.

Nancy Guthrie: Most of us are used to hearing you teach that way. So you're saying that there are settings we're not privy to in which lecturing is not your preferred method.

John Piper: Absolutely.

Nancy Guthrie: So what does it look like when you teach 1 Peter in a way that is not just a lecture?

John Piper: I walk into class, having given them, in the previous class, an assignment with maybe eight, ten, twelve verses. They are to come having analyzed those verses using a method we call "arcing." I give them study questions ahead of time. That is the hardest work. The hardest work for a teacher is writing good questions, and I think it's the key to teaching. Good questions are the key to understanding. And most teachers ask bad questions.

Nancy Guthrie: Give me an example of both a good question and a bad question.

John Piper: A bad question would be: Who are the people in this verse? What are the places in this verse? How many times does the word "of" occur in this verse? Bad questions are banal questions that don't require any thinking at all. You want a question that is hard to answer. It makes you wonder: Why is he asking that? How in the world am I going to answer that? For example, 1 Peter 3:9 says, "Do not repay evil for evil or reviling for reviling, but on the contrary, bless, for to this you were called, that you may obtain a blessing." So my question would be: Is the phrase "that you may obtain a blessing" a *motivation* for not returning evil for evil, or is it the *content* of what they were called to?

Nancy Guthrie: That's a hard question.

John Piper: That's a hard question. And not to overstate it, but a world hangs on that question—a world of how Christians should be motivated. In preparing for teaching I spend four to eight hours on those eight verses thinking of questions.

Nancy Guthrie: How many questions?

John Piper: Ten maybe. And I don't think we ever got through all the questions, because once you get them going—and that's what you want to do—get them thinking, get them talking, get them sharing their insights, get them correcting each other. Someone says, "You can't say that. It's not in the text." We're all wired to bring our experience to the text, to say what it means to *me*, and you're trying to train people not to do that but, rather, to get what it means to Peter and the reasons why it means that. The questions are all designed to push the nose down in the text so that all the answers you require have to come from the book. As soon as they start talking, and you're there shepherding that conversation to keep it from falling off a cliff on either side, it will fill up the two hours.

Nancy Guthrie: Sometimes in a Bible study discussion there are two very strong opinions about the answer to whatever the question is. And if we've asked a good question, that might be the case. Sometimes there's not just one clear or "right" answer. When you teach, are you able to resist stating the right answer, or do you want to?

John Piper: If I know with really clear arguments what I think the right answer is, I do want to, but I don't want to right away.

Nancy Guthrie: Yes, that's probably the key, isn't it, to let everyone struggle a little bit on it?

John Piper: Or a lot. I'm watching where they are in this because they've brought answers, and some are afraid to read their answers, especially if they heard a guy just give a really good answer that is different from theirs. So I'm going to pull them out, asking, "What did you write? Read it to me." This is why they have to bring written answers, because if the answers aren't written down, they'll bail on you, saying, "I didn't have time." I say, "You had time. Tell me what you wrote." Then they read it, and two or three others had the same answer, and so now he has three friends to gang up on this guy over here, and then they can start giving their reasons. And they will often wind up where I hoped they would wind up.

Nancy Guthrie: But you have to be patient.

John Piper: I have to be patient. I am a preacher, but I love *not* preaching in those settings. I love making them think, because I know preaching doesn't make the best preachers. Making people think makes the best preachers. These guys are going to be sitting some day in their study on a Friday afternoon with a sermon coming on Sunday, and they've run out of all their textual notes from seminary, and they've got to see or die. And if I haven't taught them how to see and think on their own, then they'll die. They'll quit. Or they'll just start giving stories and silly anecdotes they get from who knows where. But they won't be thrilled by what they're seeing. So my goal is to train see-ers.

Nancy Guthrie: I think some of us might rather use our time to lecture because then it's very controlled. And if we're going to turn it into a discussion, there might be disagreement. It feels a little bit like a high-wire act, and we're afraid a question is going to arise that we're not equipped to answer.

John Piper: Yes, it always does, which is very good and humbling. I could take you to a couple of texts right now that I do not know the meaning of. I'm just not God, and I want students to know they're going to see things I have not seen. I'm very greedy to know what those are. I want to be a learner. I want to be a student here.

The best teacher I ever had was Dan Fuller at Fuller Seminary. And the reason he was a good teacher (and I think he would be okay with me saying this in public) was that he was a bumbler. He would walk into class and put his notes all over the place, and he'd say, "Uh, uh, would somebody ask me a question?" I loved it! I was full of questions, and if you could just prime the pump a little bit, out would come his ideas, and I just loved it. He clearly was not intimidating. He had two PhDs and he made me feel like we could have a conversation. I took eight classes with him. Every time he opened the door, I walked in just because his pedagogical, Socratic style was explosive for me.

Nancy Guthrie: So to help us be better Bible teachers, would you say that we have to be willing to and actually have an increasing comfort with being willing to say, "I don't know"?

John Piper: Absolutely. If you've got to cover your rear end by presenting some pretense of knowledge, you'll just be a lousy teacher. That is not what teaching is about. It's about empowering. It's about releasing. It's about drawing out of people things they didn't even know were in them. If you present yourself as a know-it-all, you just shut them down. They'll be impressed, and they'll take good notes, and they'll try to do the same thing in other places. But what have you done?

I really do distinguish what my aims are for preaching and what my aims are in seminary class with sixteen guys who are going to be preachers. This is very different. You have to decide: Whom are you talking to, and what are your goals? What do you want to happen with these women? Do you want them to ape what you said out there, or do you want them to become repositories of insight because when they open their Bible they see things you never saw? That's what's happening with these guys I teach all the time. I get into conversations with them later, and they'll say something, and I say, "Whoa, I never saw that."

Nancy Guthrie: Well I guess we'd better dive into 1 Peter. I think you have to spend a little bit of time just in this greeting. When we look at it, we can't help but see Father, Son, and Spirit.

John Piper: You think that's obvious, but most people don't think when they read this: *Trinitarian introduction*. It's amazing that they're there, these early Trinitarian structures in the Bible. I think the first thing I would do is ask them what the word "according to" in verse 2 modifies. "Peter, an apostle of Jesus Christ, To those who are elect exiles of the Dispersion in Pontus, Galatia, Cappadocia, Asia, and Bithynia, *according to* . . ." What's according to? And you've got these three phrases: "*according to* the foreknowledge of God the Father, *in* the sanctification of the Spirit, *for* obedience to Jesus Christ." And then this really strange phrase, "and for sprinkling with his blood." So you have three prepositional phrases. You've got "according to" and "in" and "for." What do those all modify? This is where, if you want, to teach them sentence diagramming.

Nancy Guthrie: Do you?

John Piper: It is assumed. It's been taught before they get to me. And so I'm assuming they're doing that either in their head or on paper so that they just see it: line, subject, verb, and prepositional phrases. What are you going to put those prepositional phrases under? "According to," "of," and "for"—what will they come down from? Will it be elect? Will it be exile? Will it be both to-gether as a kind of unit? It's not an easy question. But if you don't ask that kind of question, it's kind of all hazy.

Nancy Guthrie: In Look at the Book,[1] we see you work on the text in that way. With your seminary students, do you have a board on which you are writing that? I know sometimes when I try to diagram a passage, I might come up with several stabs or possi-bilities. Is that a part of your teaching process, working together to figure that out?

---

[1] Look at the Book is a series of five- to eight-minute videos at the Desiring God website (http://desiringgod.org) in which viewers see a black screen with white text of several verses from the Bible. Viewers hear John Piper talking through the passage and see him circle and draw arrows and underline and make connections and write notes on the text with the goal of leading people through text after text to form habits of mind, habits of reading, and habits of analysis that will give people the confidence in handling the biblical text.

John Piper: Yes. Depending on where your churches are technologically, you can actually write on the new iPad Pro. I'm using it now. Or you can put a piece of paper under the projector, and that piece of paper shows upon the screen. Once upon a time they called them overheads. I did transparencies for thirty years. I would never do it in preaching. And I depart from about ten thousand preachers in that regard. Preaching to me is another kind of animal. It is a heralding moment. Thus saith the Lord. Get on your face. Hear the Lord Almighty. That is not my posture at all when I'm teaching a small group. We're just groveling around in the text trying to see everything, and something visual is really important to me.

Nancy Guthrie: We all have different learning styles. I know that for me, putting those kinds of things on the page is not busywork. It's organization that helps me understand the Holy Spirit's intended emphasis. I've got to understand his train of thought, the argument he is building.

John Piper: My brain works that way too. Typically, when I've got the text in front of me, I'll take a piece of paper and fold it in half (why I fold it in half I don't know). I use two sheets because I have a little rug on my desk, and that's because I don't like my hand on wood. It's cold. Since it's a rug, my pencil would punch right through the paper, so I have to have two sheets of paper.

Nancy Guthrie: This is a bit of a tangent, John.

John Piper: I have half sheets of paper, and I'm drawing, and I'm writing. You write "exiles," and three questions come to your mind right away. Okay, is this Jewish exiles? Is this Christians being treated like exiles? Exiles from where to where? You write those down quickly, because you're going to forget them. You will. You'll forget them in the next five seconds. They'll go right on your brain, and you'll be on to something else. So you write those down. I think C. S. Lewis said there are eyes in a pen. You start writing down a question. The pen sees possible answers. It does. They happen in your head, but it's the pen being pushed across the paper writing a question that causes the thought to come into your head. The way John Piper's brain works is that it wouldn't come into my head if I were sitting here trying to simply visualize or think three possible things. They're too jumbled in my head. So I have to get them quickly down on paper, and as I'm writing the questions about those relationships, or those prepositional phrases, or what *elect* means, what *exiles* means, possible answers come. I quickly write those down, and when I write those down I see, oh, that relates to the thing down here in the bottom left-hand corner, so I draw a line down there. So after an hour, the page is total chaos; this piece of paper is an absolute mess. Anyone would look at it and say it's garbage and to just throw it away. I say, whoa, that's an hour's worth of insight. Don't touch it. That will become a sermon.

Nancy Guthrie: I guess I would do it a little bit differently, but maybe this is part of your process too.

John Piper: There's no "right" way.

Nancy Guthrie: Before I got to writing things out on the blank page, I would print out the text in large type with plenty of space between the lines. And I'd go through it marking repeated words. I'd mark those prepositions—*according to*, *in*, *for*—and I'd be writing on the margins. There are three things that seem to be parallel. I'd put a big "exiles" and maybe make a little note asking where else do I see "exiles"? So I would be working on a page that has the text written on it.

John Piper: That is absolutely not an either-or for me. Like you, I might print it out big and write on it, but I still have this folded sheet all the time. As I work on the text, something is triggered, perhaps a flash of a relationship to Matthew 5 that can quickly disappear. So I want to capture it here.

Nancy Guthrie: If we were continuing to work through the first chapter of 1 Peter, and if we were picking up the tool of repeated words to use in the text, a number of repeated words jump out. Perhaps the most significant would have to be *salvation*. We have there in verse 9, "obtaining the outcome of your faith, the salvation of your souls. Concerning this salvation . . ." There are so many rich concepts in here—"born again to a living hope," that's one week right there. As we get into this very rich section, how are we going to determine the main place we're going with this text?

John Piper: I want the structure of the sentences to answer that question for me. I don't want to see words like *hope* or *born again*, or see words like *salvation* and, because those are big, say that they are the main point. Maybe or maybe not. The interesting thing about the way the New Testament, and really all of us, writes or talks, is that bigger realities can function as support for lesser realities, which are the main point—"main" meaning logically supported by all the others.

I should have thought through an example here in 1 Peter, but I'm thinking of one in Paul: "I am not ashamed of the gospel, for it is the power of God for salvation" (Rom. 1:16). What's the bigger reality there? Absence of shame for Paul, or the power of the gospel? No doubt the power of the gospel is the bigger reality. And it's arguing for the lesser reality. "Main point" does not mean most important reality. "Main point" means what everything else supports in this paragraph. See the difference? It's what everything else is arguing for, supporting. That may be, "Let's go eat!" And the argument may be, "I'm starving!" Well, starvation is a bigger issue than lunch, but starvation is the argument for lunch. So if you ask me how to go about deciding what to do with verses 3 through 9, I'm going to say, "Follow the train of thought and show me what he's arguing for." Where is it all going? Here, one of the biggest issues is suffering. It's almost everywhere, and when he gets to verse 6, he says "in this."

Nancy Guthrie: That's the big question: what is the "this" we are to "greatly rejoice" in?

John Piper: It's neuter in the Greek, so it doesn't refer to any of the particular words in the passage that are feminine, such as "hope." It is amazing how well you can do without knowing Greek. But it demands a lot of attention to detail, because the English will be self-correcting. For example, you don't know that the omega ("which," translated "this" in the ESV) in verse 6 is neuter, and therefore does not have a direct correlation to "inheritance," which is feminine, and "hope," which is feminine, and therefore is not referring grammatically to a specific word but to the whole box of "born again to a living hope through the resurrection of Jesus Christ from the dead, to an inheritance that is imperishable, undefiled, and unfading, kept in heaven for you, who by God's power are being guarded through faith for a salvation ready to be revealed in the last time" (1 Pet. 1:3–5). That big, glorious, new-born mercy of God-rooted inheritance is being kept—in *this* you rejoice . . . though you must suffer for a little while in order that your faith—more precious than gold—"may be found to result in praise and glory and honor at the revelation of Jesus Christ." There's the big end. Being born again is a means to that end, and having a promise of hope is a means to that end, and the suffering you're going through as a refining fire is a means to that end. You are going to come out like gold at the other end. That's where the book is going.

The book is about suffering and how to be refined by it and respond graciously and humbly in it. So I would say that new birth is a servant in this text; it's supporting other things. The promise of inheritance is a servant in this text supporting other things; it's supporting the joy of verse 6, and the joy of verse 6 is sustaining you through the suffering, and that's being sustained by the promise that you're coming out like gold refined at the other end. That's the salvation I think he's talking about here.

When you look at a paragraph like this and you want to lead these twelve women for two hours in discussing verses 3 through 9, what do you do? The key thing besides the word studies, which is absolutely crucial, is the logic. It's how the logic flows and what's being supported and what's being argued.

Nancy Guthrie: There are so many Old Testament quotations here. In chapter 1, verse 16, we've got, "You shall be holy, for I am holy," and then we've got, "For all flesh is like grass," where he goes to Isaiah. Then when we get to chapter 2, there are other quotations from Psalms. Certainly we just don't want to run over those things as if they are just part of what Peter wrote. Neither do we want to get stuck in going back too much. So help us with how to handle, especially from this section of 1 Peter, Old Testament references.

John Piper: My first question is, why do you think he did an Old Testament allusion here? And here in chapter 2 would be a good place to ask that. There's an Old Testament allusion behind verse 3: "you've tasted that the Lord is good." That is from Psalm 34:8, which is a big deal for him, because chapter 3, verses 10 to 12, are from Psalm 34, which makes you say, "Hmm, I think he liked Psalm 34." Why did he like Psalm 34? If you see three or four quotes from Psalm 34, one of your study questions might be: *Go back and read Psalm 34. What is it about this psalm that made Peter think it was relevant so that he quoted it two or three times?* I think that's a legitimate way to send them outside of 1 Peter since Peter is clearly bringing that in. So I'm asking here why this reference to Isaiah 28 is in verse 6 of chapter 2: "Behold, I'm laying in

Zion a stone," and why Psalm 118, "the stone which the builders rejected has become the cornerstone," is in 2:7. Why did he go there? Why did he refer to Jesus as a rejected stone so that whoever believes in him won't be ashamed? And I wouldn't answer it. I'd say, "You tell me."

Nancy Guthrie: Would you take everybody to those references and read through those passages?

John Piper: Yes. I'd say: "You've got a text in front of you, a footnote that tells you where this quote came from. Go back and read it." I'm asking them: what is it about the big picture of 1 Peter or chapter 2 of 1 Peter that even brings it to mind? Something brought to mind these two texts—Isaiah 28 and Psalm 118—with regard to a stone that's a stumbling stone for some, and a means of absence of shame for others, and Jesus being rejected. See what they come up with.

My answer is that I think his mind gravitated there for the same reason it gravitated to Noah in chapter 3, namely, that they are in a setting where they are a very small, beleaguered, suffering minority and are feeling rejected. They are being maligned and rejected like a stone that is considered for a building project and thrown away. He's reminding them: that is who your Savior is. You think you're being singled out for rejection? Your Savior, according to the Old Testament, was a stone rejected and made the head of the corner! That's exactly what he told them in chapter 1: "Someday you're going to shine like the sun in glory and praise and honor after you suffer for a season." I think he was pulled in that direction because he saw that. The same thing with Noah. Why would you go back and refer to preaching to eight souls, that is, eight people? Why would he draw attention to the fact that only eight people got in the ark? Because you feel like you're one of only eight believers in the Roman Empire. Or that maybe what you feel like in your town—it's just eight of us. They came safely through the water, and guess what? The whole world drowned, and he saved you.

Nancy Guthrie: In the second half of chapter 2, we begin with these numerous situations in which we are called to be in submission or subjection. And let's just be honest. As teachers, when we get to this, we start to feel uncomfortable because nobody likes the idea of submission or subjection. So we feel this sense of tension in that we want to be faithful to God's Word. We don't want to capitulate to our culture. Can you help us with that?

John Piper: When he gets to 2:12, he tells us to keep our conduct good among the Gentiles that they may glorify God. And immediately he's into submission—submission to the governing authorities, slaves' submission to masters, wives' submission to husbands, husbands loving their wives likewise. He doesn't call husbands to submit, but he does use that interesting word *likewise*. That would be one of my study questions. If there's not reciprocity here, with husbands submitting exactly the same way a wife submits, why the word *likewise*?

And then you get to 3:8, "Finally, all of you . . ." and the "all of you" are to have sympathy, brotherly love, tender heart, humble mind—the mind-set that caused citizens to go down in humility, and slaves to go down, and wives to go down, and husbands in their servant leadership to go down. This book is calling us down, down, down in servantlike humility. You are accurate to say that this is not a popular mind-set. Nor has it ever been among men or women. Nobody likes to submit to authority. That's where the world went off the rails at the beginning. We hate to be told what to do, all of us, by God or anybody—policeman, president of the United States—what bathrooms we're going to use or anything else.[2] We

---

[2] At the time of this recording, President Barack Obama had just issued a directive telling every public school district in the country to allow transgender students to use the bathrooms that match their gender identity.

don't like it. "Get off my case; I'll be my own person" is who we are by nature. So this is very counterintuitive, countercultural, counter to human nature.

Suppose you've got a lot of cool, relevant, sophisticated women in your Bible study, and they're not liking this. One of my study questions would be to focus their attention on verse 16 and ask them: What does verse 16 say about the nature of submission to government? I'd probably just leave it like that, because otherwise I might tip them off to what my answer is. It is really hard to ask questions without giving your answer away. Just after he says, "Be subject for the Lord's sake to every human institution, whether it be to the emperor as supreme, or to governors as sent by him to punish those who do evil and to praise those who do good" (2:13–14), he says in verse 16, "Live as people who are free." And you say, "Okay, what's the relationship between 'subject' and 'free,' because they sound opposite?" And they *are* opposite. If you are subjected to an authority, you're not free, are you? Well, yes, you are. This is the way I stir up discussion. I say, "Come on, how are you free? And how are you subject?"

"Live as people who are free, not using your freedom as a cover-up for evil, but living as servants of God" (1 Pet. 2:16). Okay, free, but slave of God. So who am I free in relation to? You're free in relationship to everybody—child of God, daughter of God, son of God—you are a free man. When we are born again, brought into the family of God, brought under God's perfect authority, we are nobody's slaves—not to husband, not to a parent, not to a government. We are free. Then, in that freedom, we are sent as free men and free women into structures—employment structures where you punch the clock, do what the boss says, and if you don't, you get fired. Go in there; submit. Keep the speed limit. Pay your taxes. Why? Jesus said, to paraphrase Matthew 17:25–26, "Do children pay taxes if their father is the king? No, but pay the taxes anyway."

You're all free because your Father is the owner of the universe. He owns the plantation. You're not a slave. So go work hard for the master. That's really controversial, right? What is beautiful is if you're looking to God as your authority and you're submitting yourself as a free person to this boss, this master, this policeman.

The reason I said John Piper needs 1 Peter is that I'm as rebellious as anybody. I do not like you, or my wife, or my pastor, or anybody to tell me what to do. Now, that's got to be broken. This book is about breaking the back of John Piper's rebellion until, as it says in that beautiful verse 8: "Finally, all of you, have unity of mind, sympathy, brotherly love, a tender heart, and a humble mind." Those are the things that make you able not to repay evil for evil. Last night, athlete Steph Curry lost it. He threw his mouthpiece at the ref. He lost it. He's sorry he lost it. I would have too! Five bad calls, and he lost it. This book is about that—don't lose it. If you lose it, twenty million people aren't impressed with your Christianity.

Nancy Guthrie: Over and over again in this passage he keeps telling us why we are to be subject. For example, in verse 15 it is so that we would "put to silence the ignorance of foolish people." Let's go on, because we want to try to help people who are teaching through 1 Peter, and there are a couple of passages here that are hard. As women teaching women, we get to chapter 3.

John Piper: Oh, I thought you were going to go to a hard passage.

Nancy Guthrie: As an example of wives submitting to their husbands, we read: "For this is how the holy women who hoped in God used to adorn themselves, by submitting to their own husbands, as Sarah obeyed Abraham, calling him lord. And you are her children, if you do good and do not fear anything that is frightening" (1 Pet. 3:5–6). I guess, when I think of Sarah, I don't think of her as being particularly submissive. I guess she did submit when Abraham told her to pretend that she was his sister. How do we help people understand this passage rightly? What is he pointing to when he says, "Sarah obeyed Abraham, calling him lord"?

John Piper: Before I say a word about the word "obey" there, which is really interesting, these six verses are, in my mind, the best place to go for helping women and husbands know what submission is *not*. I've preached on this maybe two or three times, and in each case I spotted six things submission is *not*. If I were teaching this class, especially to women, I would say: "I want you to go home, and I want you to bring me a list *from the text* of things that submission is *not*." And it's amazing. The wives being spoken to in this passage are trying to win their husband, which means they think he's wrong—dead wrong. So the first thing submission doesn't mean is, agree with your husband. That's a relief. We're stupid husbands who many times think things that are wrong or unhelpful. So it doesn't mean agree. Second, she's trying to win him, which means that she's trying to change him on the biggest issue in the world. So submission doesn't mean, stop trying to change your husband. This is huge when you read what Peter is saying here about what these wives are supposed to be doing in regard to their husband. With regard to the braiding of hair, the putting on of gold jewelry and clothing, if you ask why it is here, why did he go there if the issue is trying to win a husband who's not a believer by pure and chaste conduct in fear—here's my answer. It's because in many cultures, including our own, she might think: *If I could just be pretty enough, impressive enough, cool enough, sharp enough, hip enough, whatever, then I could get him to like me or want to be with me.*

Nancy Guthrie: Some women we teach think that way.

John Piper: Yeah, and so Peter is saying, "Don't go there. It's not going to work. You might get him to like you more, and it would do zero good for his soul, because he's impressed with all the wrong things. He's impressed with your hair, or your jewelry, or your clothing. So don't think that's the solution to your husband's distance from your faith. Rather, go toward this inner beauty and a gentle and quiet spirit." The word "quiet" might sound like she can never talk. And it does say to win him without a word. But clearly she needs to articulate her faith. Otherwise he doesn't know what's going on here. So I think "quiet" would be more like "tranquil." This woman is being called to something I want more than she does probably. And I say that so you'll ask, is this a uniquely feminine desirable condition of the soul? Not if you read 3:8, where it says everybody should be tenderhearted and humble minded. I want to be gentle and tranquil in my spirit. I don't want to be an anxious husband or an unkind, harsh husband. So that's the beautiful thing he's calling for. It's beautiful for men and women. And it has a peculiar beauty, I think, for a woman in a marriage relationship.

Now, to your point—"Submitting to their own husbands, as Sarah obeyed Abraham, calling him lord" (3:6). Here's where I think I would say, "Go find that in Genesis. Where did she do that?" And I might ask, as part of this question: "Why didn't he use the illustration of where Abraham told Sarah to tell the pharaoh that she was his sister because he didn't want to be killed?" This was not his shining hour. Peter didn't use that as an example of submission. He didn't. There isn't any place she calls him "lord" except in Genesis 18. I think it is where, in passing, she is talking to God and calls Abraham "my lord." It's like "sir." It's as though (and I think Schreiner takes this position in his commentary[3]) he chose a throwaway statement where she's in default mode, showing what's really in her heart by her respectful talk.

Nancy Guthrie: That's the scene where she overhears the angel saying she's going to have a child, right?

---

[3] Thomas R. Schreiner, *1, 2 Peter, Jude*, vol. 37, New American Commentary (Nashville, TN: B&H, 2007).

John Piper: Yeah. So if you ask, "Now, Peter, why did you go there to get that?" I think he would say, "This is not mainly about picking the hardest situation you can think of where a husband might ask you to do something that would be dangerous or stupid or foolish or sinful. This is about a wife's fundamental, basic disposition." What are the gears doing in the brain when they're in neutral, not when she's in control, putting it in drive or reverse? Is the wife coming out with respectful language? That's what every husband wants.

Husbands, in general, unless they're sick—and there are sick husbands—aren't after wives who are compliant in the sense that they do everything he says like a slave. This is not what marriage is and not what husbands are hungry for. Husbands do love it when their wives spontaneously say things that are upbuilding, that are commendatory and respectful. It's so interesting that that's the illustration he uses for "obey." You know what a man longs for, and you know what makes this marriage work.

The thing that makes this most preachable for a man or teachable for a woman is this last phrase: "And you are her children, if you do good" (3:6). "Do good" is part of a theme in 1 Peter. Six times we're called to "do good." So this woman is full of good deeds, and she's fearless. She's fearless. So if you are to win an unbelieving husband to Jesus, then that's the clincher. He's not going to be impressed with makeup and hair and figure—he's just not. But if you are humble on the one hand, talking him up, and free from anxieties that he's fretting about, he's not going to be able to figure you out. Why aren't you worrying about the finances? Why aren't you worrying about the kids? You want to win your husband to Jesus? Don't be a worrywart! Be fearless. This book is how to be free from fear. Don't be anxious for anything.

Nancy Guthrie: That makes me think back to the very beginning of the book where we are told that you've been born again to a living hope; you have an inheritance. Those are the kinds of things that allow us to be fearless because we're not expecting so much out of this life.

John Piper: Exactly.

Nancy Guthrie: Well, it seems really wrong not to be spending some time on "the spirits in prison" and Noah and the ark and baptism in 3:18–22. We simply don't have time for it. I've read a number of things on this, and sometimes they differ. Maybe you could point us to a resource or two.

John Piper: And the same thing about preaching to the dead in 4:6. Those are the two patches I was referring to when I said I don't know what they mean. I have two interpretations in my mind that vie for the upper hand. The two commentaries I would recommend for them are Grudem and Schreiner.[4] They're both manageable if you don't have Greek, which I assume some do, but most don't perhaps. That's where I would go.

In regard to this particular issue, I don't think I'd recommend any particular article or anything, but I would just say, try to stand back from the details of this really puzzling text and just ask the bigger-picture questions. Did Christ preach to the dead, or did he preach in the day of Noah by the Holy Spirit to those who are now dead? Those are the two main views. I go back and forth based on who I read, because there are pretty good arguments both ways. I lean toward thinking Jesus, in the Spirit, went and preached to the saints in the days of Noah, because that's what chapter 1 says. It makes sense for why it would belong in 1 Peter. I'm not sure why he would even bother with it if he were saying that between the death of Jesus and the resurrection, Jesus went to Hades and preached and liberated the souls. I'm just not sure why that would help in the text, but I'm not going to be dogmatic about that. If

---

[4] Wayne Grudem, *1 Peter*, Tyndale, vol. 17, New Testament Commentaries (Downers Grove, IL: IVP Academic, 2009); and Schreiner, *1, 2 Peter, Jude.*

people come with really strong views, saying, "He descended into hell. It's in the Apostles' Creed. That's where they get it," I think, okay, but that might not be what it means.

Nancy Guthrie: When 1 Peter comes to an end, Peter says, "I've written briefly to you, exhorting and declaring that this is the true grace of God. Stand firm in it" (5:12). We are people who really want, when we teach the Bible, those who hear it to hear the true grace of God. But there are a lot of hard words in this book. Would you help us know what's it going to look like for us to declare the true grace of God and to stand firm in it as teachers of the Bible?

John Piper: I would, if I hadn't done it already, make one of my study questions to find all the uses of the word *grace*. I would encourage everyone in my class to have a Bible software program on their computer—something simple or big—Logos is big; Bibleworks is big; Accordance is big.[5] And there are others. I think everybody today should probably work in one, because it makes word study so easy. Just click on "grace" and there are three or four occurrences. Read all of them in context and bring back what you think true grace is. He began that way when he said, "Concerning this salvation, the prophets who prophesied *about the grace* that was to be yours" (1:10); and in chapter 2, "But if when you do good and suffer for it you endure, this is *a gracious thing* in the sight of God" (2:20). When you are beaten for it and don't strike back, it is a beautiful grace.

Grace is a really big, future-oriented-with-present-implications term. So I'd get them to read all those texts. Then I would take that "stand firm in it" and say, "What in 1 Peter are illustrations of standing firm in it?" The closest one is, "the devil prowls around like a roaring lion, seeking someone to devour. Resist him, firm in your faith" (5:8–9). So I think the "stand firm" here means to believe

---

[5] For more information on these resources, see https://www.logos.com; http://www.bibleworks .com; and http://www.accordancebible.com.

the promises he's made, believe the future that he's held out to you, believe that he cares for you. It's believing these glorious things that creates the firmness of the standing. And that creates the fearlessness of the wife in the marriage to an unbelieving husband that makes the husband say, "I can't figure you out."

Nancy Guthrie: That's something we want to be teaching to others, but it's also something we need too as teachers. We need the true grace of God to impact us deeply, to become a part of us so that it becomes a part of our words. We want to be teachers who stand firm in the grace of God.

John Piper: Yeah. And it's intention. Those two words are intention, aren't they, because "standing firm" sounds like an oak tree, not like teeny petals of a rose, but oaks of righteousness standing, whereas "grace" sounds like blessing the people who are hurting you. You're not returning evil for evil. You're blessing them, and that's grace. So we've been mistreated; we stand like a rock in it, knowing that "I'm accepted, I'm loved because he treated me better than I deserve. Now this maligning is coming against me. Will I be gracious? Will the grace go out?"

Nancy Guthrie: Thank you, Dr. Piper, for helping us teach the Bible.

Contributors

D. A. Carson

D. A. Carson (PhD, University of Cambridge) is cofounder and president of the Gospel Coalition and since 1978 has taught at Trinity Evangelical Divinity School (Deerfield, Illinois), where he currently serves as Research Professor of New Testament. He came to Trinity from Northwest Baptist Theological Seminary in Vancouver, British Columbia, and has served in pastoral ministry in Canada and the United Kingdom. He and his wife, Joy, have two children.

Nancy Guthrie

Nancy Guthrie speaks at conferences around the country and internationally, has authored numerous books, and hosts a podcast series, "Help Me Teach the Bible." She and her husband, David, live in Nashville. They are cohosts of the GriefShare video series used in more than eighty-five hundred churches around the country and host Respite Retreats for couples who have experienced the death of a child.

Kathleen Nielson

Kathleen Nielson (PhD, Vanderbilt University) is senior adviser and book editor for the Gospel Coalition. She has taught English, directed Bible studies, speaks and writes extensively, and loves studying the Bible with women. Kathleen and her husband, Niel, live partly in Wheaton, Illinois, and partly in Jakarta, Indonesia. They have three sons, two daughters-in-law, and five granddaughters.

John Piper

John Piper (DTh, University of Munich) is founder and teacher of Desiring God (DesiringGod.org), and chancellor of Bethlehem College & Seminary in Minneapolis, Minnesota. He is a founding Council member of the Gospel Coalition. For thirty-three years, he served as senior pastor at Bethlehem Baptist Church. He and his wife, Noël, have four sons, one daughter, and a growing number of grandchildren.

Carrie Sandom

Carrie Sandom (BTh, University of Oxford) serves as director of women's ministry for the Proclamation Trust in the UK and trains women for Bible teaching ministry at London's Cornhill Training Course. She worked with students in Cambridge and young professionals in London before moving to St. John's, Tunbridge Wells, where she works with women of all ages and stages of life.

Jen Wilkin

Jen Wilkin is a speaker, author, and teacher of women's Bible studies in Dallas, Texas. She has organized and led studies for women in home, church, and parachurch contexts. Her passion is to see women become articulate and committed followers of Christ, with a clear understanding of why they believe what they believe and grounded in the Word of God. You can find her at jenwilkin.net.

Mary Willson

Mary Willson serves as the director of women's initiatives for the Gospel Coalition and is presently engaged in doctoral studies on the Old Testament at Trinity Evangelical Divinity School. She also holds an MDiv and ThM from Gordon-Conwell Theological Seminary. Alongside her academic work, she enjoys teaching and training others to teach the Scriptures, especially in the context of the local church. She has many nieces and nephews who make life all the more wonderful and rambunctious.

General Index

of (hope fully, be holy, fear rightly, love earnestly), 60–61; and Jesus in Caesarea Philippi, 131–32; knowledge of Scripture, 14–18; personal story of, 77–78; view of divine inspiration, 13–14; view of Scripture, 13–14. *See also* 1 Peter
priesthood, holy, 85, 93; our collective identity as, 84
Prince George, 80, 93
professional life, 107–11

rejection, 27–28; our Savior rejected by men, 27
Rome, as Babylon, 42
Roseveare, Helen, 51–52

salvation, 19, 21–23, 46, 54; accomplishment of by the Triune God, 22; the privileged salvation of Israel, 22–23
Sanchez, Juan, 87
Sarah, 31, 113, 178–79, 180
Scripture, 37–38
Sermon on the Mount, 103n1
servanthood, 151–52
sin, 69; doctrine of, 140; forgiveness of, 23; slavery of, 25; understanding the consequences of, 62
slavery, in the first century, 107, 110n6
sober-mindedness, 62–63
spiritual house, the, building of, 82
Stockdale, James, 47–48, 47n1

Stockdale Paradox, the, 47, 49–50
submission, 31n12, 107–8; to governing authorities, 30; of servants to masters, 30; of wives to unbelieving husbands, 30–31
suffering, 38, 39, 173–74; of the body of Christ, 50; of Christ, 33; of Job, 157; as part of God's plan, 53; purpose of, 33–34; role of Satan in, 156–57. *See also* suffering/persecution, of Christians
suffering/persecution, of Christians, 121–24; and God's will, 128–29; and hope, 126–27; persecution as a cause of rejoicing, 141–43, 148; persecution should never come as a surprise to Christians, 140–41; persecution should never come to us as a result of evil done by Christians, 143; as a privilege, 143; and serving, 149–50; as a step in the purification of Christians, 143–44; suffering for what is right, 125–26; view of within the framework of God's providential rule over Christians, 144; and witnessing, 127–28. *See also* suffering/persecution, of Christians, and the role of Christ

Scripture Index

THE GOSPEL **COALITION**

The Gospel Coalition is a fellowship of evangelical churches deeply committed to renewing our faith in the gospel of Christ and to reforming our ministry practices to conform fully to the Scriptures. We have committed ourselves to invigorating churches with new hope and compelling joy based on the promises received by grace alone through faith alone in Christ alone.

We desire to champion the gospel with clarity, compassion, courage, and joy—gladly linking hearts with fellow believers across denominational, ethnic, and class lines. We yearn to work with all who, in addition to embracing our confession and theological vision for ministry, seek the lordship of Christ over the whole of life with unabashed hope in the power of the Holy Spirit to transform individuals, communities, and cultures.

Through its women's initiatives, The Gospel Coalition aims to support the growth of women in faithfully studying and sharing the Scriptures; in actively loving and serving the church; and in spreading the gospel of Jesus Christ in all their callings.

Join the cause and visit TGC.org for fresh resources that will equip you to love God with all your heart, soul, mind, and strength, and to love your neighbor as yourself.

TGC.org

Also Available from the Gospel Coalition

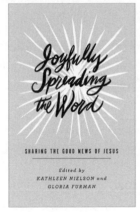
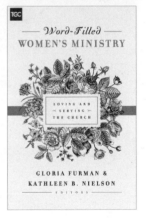

For more information, visit crossway.org.